WALTer Grass

CODE
OF ETHICS

By

H. B. MONJAR

NEW YORK
THE KEY PUBLISHING CO., INC.
PUBLISHERS

Printed in the United States of America

To My Friends

In The

MANTLE CLUB

This Book

Is Affectionately Dedicated

INTRODUCTION

IN compiling the following articles and arranging them in book form the Author is actuated by a growing demand for these monthly articles in a more convenient form for reference, and a sincere desire to encourage the use of a practical Code of Ethics which can be translated into the life and actions of the average American citizen.

These articles are not meant to be learned dissertations for the selected few but are written for the help and guidance of all decent and respectable citizens. The Author feels that one of the principal uses of intelligence is to convey an understandable message to those who have not been fortunate enough to have an extended education or comparable practical experience; and that real intelligence should be used to educate individuals and gradually increase their ability to understand and apply principles; and that it is a false and misleading method to write in a manner that only a specially selected few can understand when the message is intended for general use.

Therefore these articles have been written in order to reach the understanding of children as well as educated adults of exceptional intelligence and with the hope that a comprehensive and simple Code of Ethics will in time become a compulsory part of the curriculum of our institutions of learning; and that every child will be instructed from the time of entering school in the fundamental traits of character that are so much more vitally important than any of the academic or technical subjects which might be taught.

These addresses were written monthly to the members of an organization which has for one of its chief purposes the betterment of character and another purpose which is almost as vital, that being the welfare and happiness of all loyal American citizens. It is only fitting, therefore, that the preliminary introduction as made by the Author at the time should be made a part of this permanent record. For the reader's benefit the following lines are quoted verbatim:

"This is the first of a series of messages intended for use at the regular monthly meetings of the organization. It is my desire to use this method in order that we may all be drawn closer to one another in a spirit of true friendliness and helpful association. You all know the general purposes of the organization and you also understand the necessary qualifications for membership. It is my hope to bring out in more vivid detail the spirit, romance, adventure and hope that pertain to the organization as well as the possibilities of pleasant and profitable association, of protection at all times, of help in time of need and of strict justice under all conditions.

This is not merely a fraternal organization. It is a strong and sturdy vehicle to carry us along the road to safety, content, and happiness, when our own powers of progress fail or become diminished. It is a light to shine upon the road that leads not only to a fuller and more successful life but to a better one. The path of duty and of the right course of action may often seem hard and almost impossible to follow but this is almost always when we are treading this path alone. Surrounded by friends the path no longer seems hard or impossible. It then becomes an adventure, full not only of hope and promise for the future, but full of certainty, comfort, protection, and pleasure in the present. Loneliness becomes no longer a thing of dread or fear, for those who walk with true and loyal friends can never be alone, altho at times they may temporarily be separated. Even at such times, however, the spirit, courage, and friendship of the group constitute a source of unfailing strength to the individual. With loneliness gone, fear banished, and security assured the path of life becomes a pleasant and steady progress from whatever point an individual might enter thereon.

The goal of happiness lies within the heart, mind, and body of an individual and therefore has to be obtained by the individual in person, but in almost every case it requires the help and assistance of a guiding hand, of friendly counsel, of personal interest in the individual, and of companionship of others who are guided by the same principles and actuated by the same motives. It is my purpose to go into detail later on as to the qualities necessary to attain happiness and success in its true form. I desire here to merely enumerate the qualities that go to make up a dependable and reliable individual.

This organization is interested in the practical application of ideals and principles and I have therefore brought out not only the explanation of these qualities from an ethical standpoint, which has to do with moral right and moral wrong, but have also mentioned the practical application of such qualities to the business world of which we are all a part."

THE AUTHOR

MARCH 1st, 1938.

Contents

Article	Title	Page
I	Character Traits	1
II	Honor	6
III	Loyalty	12
IV	Common Sense	17
V	Courage	22
VI	Justice	28
VII	Ambition and Pride	36
VIII	Self-Control	42
IX	Self-Control	49
X	Confidence	55
XI	Energy	61
XII	Reliability	68
XIII	Responsibility	75
XIV	Reason	82
XV	Independence	89
XVI	Self-Respect	97
XVII	Strength	102
XVIII	Comparisons	110
XIX	Appreciation	120
XX	Decision	127
XXI	Importance	135
XXII	Truth	144

Article	Title	Page
XXIII	Perseverance	154
XXIV	Adaptation	165
XXV	Caution	170
XXVI	Companionship	175
XXVII	Values	182
XXVIII	Fair Play	188

CHARACTER TRAITS

HONOR

HONOR is the quality that inspires a man to be not merely honest, but to use the highest principles in his personal and business conduct because of his inherent desire to do only those things that are right and just and worth while. Honesty is, in many cases, inspired by outside influences such as fear, etc., while honor comes from within and is one of the necessary qualities for permanent building of manhood in its best sense. It is essential to places of trust and confidence in the business world.

LOYALTY

Loyalty is one of the most desirable qualities to be found in any individual. Our first loyalty, supreme above all, is loyalty to God, to Country, to our homes, and to our self-respect. In the very nature of things these loyalties can never conflict with each other, if we are really thinking along just and honest lines. Our loyalty also belongs to our loved ones, our friends, our communities, and last but by no means least to the whole of mankind. Loyalty does not condone wrongdoing or attempt to minimize its punishment. Loyalty remains a friendly and helping hand in adversity or time of trouble regardless of the individual's own part in bringing about such situations. True loyalty does not lend itself to help in evading justified punishment, but does lend itself to aid the individual in overcoming the obstacles that present themselves while justice is being meted out or after it has been satisfied. Loyalty to principles should only change when higher or better principles are available as substitutes. Loyalty to leaders should be given only so long as their characters and adherence to principles justify such loyalty, but care should be taken to see that unproved charges against any individual are never used as an excuse for disloyalty.

Loyalty requires that every man should give his full measure of ability and careful thought to his work whether he likes it or dislikes it, whether his efforts are appreciated or unappreciated, in order to prove true to his own best interests, both as to the upbuilding of character and the acquiring of the ability to work under adverse conditions. He should be sincerely loyal to his employers and give them more than a fair return for compensation received. Every business institution must make a profit on each employe to justify his retention, for it is the profits made by employes that alone justify continuing business.

COMMON SENSE

Common sense is essential in all walks of life, in the home, in the family, in the community, in dealings with our friends and acquaintances, and in social, political and business activities. Common sense can probably be best explained by saying it means giving fair play and a square deal to everybody, including yourself. To fight for other people's rights with the vigor that you would fight for your own and to fight for your own rights with determination from the standpoint of justice if not desire.

Common sense is the steering wheel that keeps a man on the high road between the cliffs of impractical ideals on the one hand and the abyss of loose living and lack of high principles on the other. This high road in business is the road to success. The cliffs represent impractical and visionary schemes with especial reference to those which appeal to an individual's desire to get something for nothing, or at least without adequate effort. The abyss represents fear, hopelessness and pessimism in the order named and unless a man eradicates these qualities, he is sure to end in oblivion so far as success in the business world is concerned. Common sense can and should be applied by an intelligent man to every problem in life, but it is absolutely vital in business problems.

COURAGE

Courage is the quality that enables men to willingly give up their lives for those things they know to be right. It is absolutely necessary for either contentment or happiness. Courage is of three kinds, moral, mental, and physical. Physical courage is desirable as physical fear makes happiness impossible, but mental and moral courage are far more important. Mental courage has to do with wisdom and moral courage has to do with right and wrong and is covered by ethical standards.

In the business world it is the quality that inspires men to start things, to take the necessary risks of pioneering or to launch in business for themselves. Courage must not be spasmodic for it is essential that anything that is started should be carried through to a successful conclusion. This naturally requires a permanent battle against obstacles; therefore the quality of courage must be permanent and enduring. A man may have his moments of depression but he should never be hampered by fear.

JUSTICE

Justice is a quality which we continually strive for but can never attain in full measure. The best each of us can do is to strive for it with all our might. It is useless to try to discuss the ethical qualities pertaining to justice in a short article, therefore this particular subject will be discussed in great detail in due order.

In the business world this particular quality can be considered as being the one which causes our business relations with others to be profitable to them as well as to ourselves. This mutuality of profit must be considered as vital by the man who desires a permanent and enduring success.

AMBITION AND PRIDE

Ambition and pride of the right kind are also necessary. Ambition to be of real service to the world and to be well thought of for qualities which are actually possessed by the individual; pride in the fact that he keeps his word and his own self-respect as well as the respect of others.

SELF-CONTROL

Self-control is the quality that prescribes temperance in all things, in speech, in thought and in actions. Every intelligent man readily accepts this fact, but few actually act upon it. To help each member to translate his wisdom of thought into wisdom of action is one of the chief aims of the organization. In the business world it is essentially important.

CONFIDENCE

Confidence is necessary for agreeable relations with our fellow men. It is also necessary to content and happiness. It is a mutual transaction in its really perfect form. Those who have no confidence in others should not expect others to have confidence in them. This does not mean that confidence is bestowed upon unworthy or dishonest individuals. On the other hand it does not mean that every one is to be suspected of dishonest intentions merely because you do not know them or their background. Confidence requires a general belief in the good intentions and general honesty of other people, but common sense is required in all transactions, with friends as well as with strangers, in order that no harm may be done, regardless of the good or evil intentions of the other party to a transaction. It is the cornerstone of the structure of business activities. Without it, business of the present day world could not be transacted. It should be safeguarded, however, against those who would use it for the purpose of fraud, and common sense has to determine our course of action along such lines.

ENERGY

Energy is necessary for full success in our personal lives but especially in business. We use the word energy instead of health as many individuals in reasonably good health do not demonstrate the energy that is necessary to progress, while others in poor health have demonstrated unusual energy of mind and body. A sound mind in a sound body can be attained by the large majority of individuals if they are actually desired by them. No man who desires success should fail to keep himself in good sound physical and mental condition.

June, 1934

HONOR

HONOR is an all-embracing quality and it can almost truly be said that an honorable man is necessarily endowed with most of the other important and worth while qualities of real manhood. It takes moral courage of the highest quality to be honorable at all times and under all circumstances. We cannot consider a man as really honorable unless he has the quality of loyalty. Justice also is a necessary attribute of the honorable man. It is also hard to conceive of a man possessed of a high sense of honor not also possessing ambition and pride of the right kind. Self-control is necessary to enable a man to carry out his honorable intentions. Confidence in himself and in others implies strength of character and no man can be truly honorable without also being strong. It is quite true that health of body is not necessarily a part of the picture, but the health of a man's mind and of his morals are necessary, therefore energy as we use it, is a part of the characteristics of an honorable man. Last, but not least, common sense is vitally necessary in order to enable the use of good judgment as to the honorable course to follow.

Honor is a quality that is universally respected even by the most vicious elements. It is a word that has never been dragged in the dirt or subjected to criticism. It is perfectly true that the hypocritical assumption of honor has been criticised severely but this only emphasizes the real reverence and respect that is held by practically every individual for the quality of honor itself. Criminals even apply to certain law enforcement officials the name of "straight shooter" to designate this quality. They mean particularly that they can rely upon his word and that they know he will give them a square deal, no more and no less. In the business world the same qualities of personal integrity due to the inner promptings of the man's own nature are recognized by the assumption that such a man's word is absolutely to be relied upon and that he will always deal fairly and squarely without seeking an undue or unjust advantage. It is the same in all walks of life, therefore honor denotes dependability and reliability that is practically absolute from an ethical standpoint.

We desire, however, to call attention to a very vital phase of this important quality. There has been a tendency ever since the beginning of recorded history for men to remove themselves from the stress and temptation of general affairs in order that they might live honorable lives. Many men and women have refrained from assuming responsibilities and from striving to better their own conditions and the conditions of their fellow men and women because of fear that such activities would interfere with their ability to lead honorable and upright lives. In honor we have an instrument that is given us to use, not only to enable each of us as an individual to lead the right kind of life, but also particularly to inspire and help others to do the same and to set them the proper example. This quality therefore should be made use of to the full extent of the ability of the individual and to fail to do this is to fail to live up to our responsibilities to the Creator who placed this quality in our possession and for our own use.

It is a comparatively simple matter for a man or woman to isolate themselves from contact with the world and thus to remove themselves from most of the temptations human flesh is heir to, but this denotes weakness and not the strength of character that is going to be helpful to others. It is the same as saying that they can be honorable if removed from temptation, but that they doubt their ability to live up to their standards under normal conditions. The average man is forced to live in a work-a-day world and it is practically a sacred duty for him to aspire to and strive for the greatest attainments of which he is capable along the lines of his abilities and in the right channels. It is significant therefore that if we have merely the desire to benefit ourselves from an ethical standpoint, that we can be mildly and unobtrusively honorable and to such men as desire to attain this particular goal only, full credit must be given for their attainment. But men who really desire to be of benefit to the world and to help others as well as themselves must necessarily show that it is possible to keep and make effective this quality of honor in the highest places and in the most important activities of the nation and of the world.

Honesty in its strict sense has to do with legal justice and with absolute truth in our personal lives, while honor comes from within and goes far beyond honesty and personal integrity. Honor concerns itself not only with a decision as to what is the right thing to do but more importantly with seeing that it is done, so far as lies within the power of the individual. A truly honorable man in loyalty to his country and to his community should exercise his franchise whenever possible and do his part in electing to office men whose word can be trusted and who will give all the people fair play and a square deal. He must of necessity be loyal to his country and to its welfare, but its welfare should be rated in importance as spiritual, mental and physical. He should do all in his power to see that his country or his community through its elected officials keep their word and obligations and deal fairly and justly with all individuals alike whether they be citizens of our own nation or of other nations.

No physical benefit should be allowed to interfere as to carrying out the moral and legal obligations of our government. To do so is to sell our birthright for a mess of pottage. The present troubled condition of the world in general is caused by lack of faith between the nations of the world and between various classes of citizens in these nations. There is a striving for group advantage to the benefit of themselves and to the detriment of others. Nations break their word with impunity when they so desire and they give as an excuse that it is necessary to the welfare of their own people. Of course every human being really knows that the welfare of the people demands that the nation keep its honorable obligations, or in case of inability to do so arrange to take care of them in the future. The nation is a composite body representing all of the people and the citizens of every nation are entitled to know beyond doubt that their government sets its standard of honor at least as high as the standard of honor pertaining to individuals. It is increasingly necessary therefore that high-minded and right-thinking citizens use all of their ability and intelligence not only to maintain this standard of honor in their own personal, business, and social affairs, but that they should fight for it as an accepted standard of conduct on the part of other individuals, of the community, the state, the nation and the world.

It is the duty of intelligent men to do their part to see that this standard is maintained and upheld and gradually to transmit to others the effects created by our own example. In order that we may do this successfully it is necessary, in exercising judgment as to the honorable course to follow, to be extremely careful to avoid mistakes of judgment due to our personal desires, personal benefits, and our personal prejudices. At a later date it is our intention to write a special message in regard to the formulation of a correct viewpoint on the part of individuals, as it covers too much territory to be formulated within the scope of a few paragraphs. For the present it is sufficient to say that even the average conscientious individual makes mistakes of judgment in matters where he is personally concerned, in most cases being totally unaware of the fact that he is allowing his personal interest to sway his judgment. A large majority of thinking men and women are perfectly capable of advising the right course of action on the part of others in a given set of circumstances, but given the same circumstances, where it affects them personally, they sometimes act in absolute opposition to the course of procedure that they would unhesitatingly recommend to others. Very many of the problems that confront the average high-minded individual are problems that he hesitates to mention to anyone else because of their confidential nature. The only satisfactory solution is for each man to be honest with himself, to try to figure out what he would recommend to another man as the right course of action under similar circumstances, and to proceed accordingly without regard to his own desires or even his own interests.

A man has no more cherished possession than honor and he should guard it carefully against all assaults. It should never be weighed in the balance as against personal desire or benefit. Without honor a man can never hope to attain happiness, and personal success becomes a delusion and a snare. Honor is the seed from which the tree of happiness springs. The root represents strength of character, the tree being no stronger and no more full of life than its root. The body of the tree represents the man himself, anchored by strength, founded on honor, living and expanding year by year in the practical everyday world, which is represented by the soil in which it grows. The fruit and foliage of the tree represent happiness.

The tree may be small or large, it may be a fruit or a shade tree, it may live long or die an early death, but if it fulfills the purpose for which it was created it will have done its duty, made the world a little better and brighter place in which to live, and have brought some happiness to others.

June, 1934

LOYALTY

IN spite of the fact that the quality of loyalty is highly respected and held in great esteem by practically all individuals regardless of their general character, it is a much misused word, and in many cases is a cover for selfish inclinations of the individual. Specifically, loyalty in its generally accepted meaning, means to be true, and this carries with it the obligation of being just and right. Loyalty can mistakenly be given to principles and activities that are incorrect or wrong from the standpoint of ethics and morals, but never with the knowledge of the individual that these things are true in regard to such principles and activities. In other words adherence to wrong principles of thought, speech and action is not loyalty in any sense of the word, but is inspired by selfish and unworthy motives. This can be generally understood by the average thinking man or woman, but when we come to the field of personal loyalty a great many otherwise intelligent individuals become confused and uncertain.

The criminal element feels that loyalty demands obstruction of justice, even to the extent of committing other and greater crimes in protecting those who deserve punishment. Going to the other extreme we find that many high-minded individuals believe that loyalty to their convictions in regard to right principles should impel them to refrain from defense of their own country in case of war. The answer to this problem, given by Christ Himself, in reply to questions which were propounded in order that He might be accused of disloyalty to the government, was very simple, "Render unto Caesar the things that are Caesar's, and unto God the things that are God's."

The loyal citizen must have a greater loyalty to his country and to its laws than he has to any individual, or group, and his first loyalty must be to his God and Country. Loyalty to God cannot interfere with loyalty to your own country. It does not interfere with loyalty to its rulers except where it is ruled by tyrants who usurp the prerogatives of God Himself. Those who crush the liberties of the people are never entitled to loyalty and it should not be given to them. The so-called "Pacifist" who does not believe in what he calls legalized murder or war, has a perfect right to his convictions, but he cannot hide behind the skirts of these convictions to avoid defending his country when necessity arises. It is quite true that war is objectionable in its every feature and horrible in many of them, but it is impossible to protect the world, and especially our loved ones, against criminality and brute force except by opposition with a greater force and power. The individual who will not fight in defense of his loved ones and of his own country, maintains this attitude in practically all cases because he is not personally endangered (and as an added incentive he doesn't desire to be), yet it is only the men who fight that make it safe for those who stay at home. All of the sophistry used as arguments against war are of but little avail so long as there are powerful nations who desire to subjugate or conquer other nations. It is the duty of all right-minded individuals to do all in their power to bring about and make permanent a friendly spirit between the nations of the world, but it is unsafe and idiotic for any nation to practice the policy of nonresistance. Does anyone really believe that the boys who fought in the trenches in the world war believed in the policy of killing each other, or that they were any less high-minded than those who claimed exemption or secured it by some underhand method? Practically no one engaged in the war believed in this policy of killing, it was only that each soldier or sailor felt that he was fighting in defense of his own country, that made it possible for the war to continue. Loyalty to God requires the protection of loved ones, who are defenseless and helpless, and not their enemies. The only way that war will ever be stopped is by loyalty given to the word of honor of each and every nation. So long as nations are willing to break their agreements, war cannot possibly be stopped. True loyalty, therefore, to principles, with a common and mutual interest and benefit to all nations, is the only effective means of preventing conflict.

Loyalty to individuals must first be given from the standpoint of the best interest of the individual. This means that, if the individual *should* be punished, your loyalty to the individual requires that this punishment should be meted out and that you do nothing to obstruct such punishment. On the other hand if the individual is innocent and should *not* be punished, then you should move heaven and earth if necessary to avoid such punishment, doing everything that is honorable and legal to attain that end. It is not loyalty but selfishness that prompts individuals to side with those that they know to be in the wrong, and this personal prejudice and selfish attitude should never be dignified by the name of loyalty. Unfounded charges, slander, gossip and malicious innuendos, are never sufficient reason for withdrawal of loyalty. The true facts should be ascertained, and these *facts* should determine whether our loyalty is justified or otherwise. These facts should be ascertained, however, in a manner that will not humiliate, hurt, or embarrass the individual accused, in the event that he is innocent of the charges. He should always be presumed innocent until the facts themselves prove him guilty. Another very important feature of judgment in such cases has to do with the manner in which charges are presented. Many individuals have been condemned for doing things that were perfectly legal and honorable and that should not have even been criticized, the charges being presented in such manner as to imply that these acts were dishonorable or illegal. It is the duty of each individual not only to determine whether the acts themselves are dishonorable or illegal, but also whether they are sufficient cause for withdrawing his loyalty. The attitude of the man committing such acts must largely determine the final judgment. Mistakes are frequently made on questions of honor or legality, but it is the intent and purpose behind the act that should be most carefully considered. It is regrettably true that disloyalty to those to whom we were previously loyal has been caused far more by unproved falsehoods and slander, than by any actual act or deed of the individual concerned.

We have a loyalty to God, to our Country, to our loved ones and to principles, but we also have a loyalty to our business associates, our employers and our employes. An employer should take a personal interest in providing steady, continuous and profitable employment, and the employe should take a personal interest in doing everything in his power to bring about profits and progress for the institution that pays him his salary or wage. The fact that other individuals are disloyal can never be used as a means of covering up or mitigating our own disloyalty. If a man forsakes loyalty to his Creator he should openly proclaim the fact, so that everyone can classify him where he belongs. If he is willing to be disloyal to his Country, then he should remove himself to some other country to which he feels he could give his loyalty. If an employer is not really loyal to the welfare of his men, he should be prevented from holding down his high position, regardless of his financial interest, and another should be substituted in his place to actually handle the men under his jurisdiction. If an employe feels that he cannot give his loyalty to his employer's interests, he should at once remove himself from his affiliation and not become a traitor to his own sense of honor. If a man feels that he should forsake his loyalty to anyone he has previously loved, to a previous friend, to certain leaders, or to a group or institution, he should make perfectly clear that he is abandoning his loyalty because of proven facts that justify such action, or he should classify himself as one who abandons loyalty on hearsay evidence, or on suspicion, and thereby make known to everyone that his loyalty is of no importance to anyone, for the simple reason that in such a man loyalty does not really exist.

Loyalty to principles requires steady and persistent application. If a man is really honest with himself, high principles do not conflict with each other, but on the contrary re-enforce each other. If a man has high principles and he steadily adheres to them as a guide, he can safely be trusted to give his loyalty where it belongs and in the way that it should be given. Those who become confused inevitably do because of personal desire, personal profit, prejudice, or ignorance. Those who follow the guidance of high principles can really never be uncertain about their duty in regard to loyalty.

July, 1934

COMMON SENSE

COMMON SENSE is variously labeled reason, intelligence, instinct and sometimes intuition, and those who have the least of this remarkable quality are usually those who praise it so highly, believing mistakenly that they have a large share of it in their own character.

Common sense is often distorted into meaning a very low grade of reason, in other words the sense that is common to practically everyone. This is totally untrue. Common sense is one of the rarest traits of character in its application, that is to be found. Common sense consists of being able to see facts clearly, without interference because of prejudice or personal interest, and consequent action in harmony with the established facts.

Common sense is a dual trait of character. It consists of seeing facts and acting upon them. To see facts and not to act upon them is to play the part of an ignorant individual, and to act without understanding the facts is pure folly.

The reason why the term common sense has been applied to this particular trait of character is because practically every reasonably intelligent individual can actually see and understand the facts about most of the problems of life. When they fail to do so it is practically always because of their personal prejudice, selfishness, or a desire to evade responsibility. They willfully blind themselves in such cases to what they could readily understand if they were seeking only for the truth, therefore common sense as representing the actual ability of the average man or woman to see and understand facts is truly a common and general attribute and is therefore rightly termed.

The use of this quality, however, in its full measure is restricted to a very limited number of individuals and it is not therefore actually practiced sufficiently to be called common.

We can liken the average individual to a baseball player of great ability in hitting who merely stands at the plate and watches the ball, but makes no attempt to hit it except in spasmodic intervals and then only in a half-hearted manner. How much success a man can make of his life can be readily estimated by the success that would attend such a ball player if he acted in the manner described above. This is probably one of the most potent reasons why so few individuals actually attain success, from the standpoint of respect and good will of their fellow men, as well as financial and business standing.

Common sense requires that fair play and justice be considered at all times in relation to actual facts and the consequent action thereon. It is not intended for the purpose of telling other people what to do unless our advice is actually requested with sincerity, but is a guide to our own individual actions both in carrying out our own individual responsibilities and in directing those who are under our guidance and control.

Common sense requires that each individual citizen should exercise his franchise in order that the rule of the people should be perpetuated. Common sense dictates a temperate attitude regarding everything except principles, ethics, and morals.

Common sense dictates that you keep your nose out of other people's business, and that you give diligent attention to your own, but this does not mean that each citizen should not fight continuously for the preservation of the rights and liberties of the general public, as that is actually a part of his business of being a citizen. The citizen who fights vigorously for his own rights may often get more than his share, but this in the long run does not contribute to the welfare of the large body of citizens. Common sense dictates organized effort and cooperation on the part of the whole people to see that their government is properly managed.

In social and business life individuals should endeavor to eliminate either a superiority or inferiority complex. The gracious lady and the aristocratic gentleman who are so condescending and superior in their attitude are just as obnoxious and as little actuated by common sense as the ignorant hoodlum, and the unrefined and unambitious individual of little brains and no responsibility.

It is not necessary to have a real appreciation of either very classical music, such as some grand operas, or to enjoy the most vicious forms of jazz music, in order to be a real music lover in an intelligent way.

Common sense dictates that the average man and woman should marry and have children, but this does not mean that they should get married half a dozen times, or have two or three dozen children. Moderation is the essence of common sense. We should neither eat too much food, nor too little food. We should have enough clothes, but not so much it constitutes a burden. We should have a home large enough for comfort and convenience, but not so large that the homelike quality is banished.

Especially in regard to other people's likes and dislikes, tastes and beliefs, should we use common sense. There should be tolerance and appreciation of other people's sincere convictions, whether of religion, politics, or otherwise. Personal habits of other individuals should not be criticized unless they are actually offensive, distasteful, or obnoxious. Above all common sense commands that you should not attempt to make other people over to suit your own standards, except through advice and helpful guidance, and that you should not allow other people to make you over according to their standards unless you are entirely convinced that their standards are higher and better than your own.

Common sense must be dependable as a permanent trait of character, it cannot be used one day or one time and discarded at another, with any degree of satisfaction. Children and adults should both be properly punished for wrongdoing, but the proper punishment has to do with the nature and temperament of the individual and no set of laws can be made that will have the proper effect on all human beings.

Some motor car drivers can drive carefully at a rate of forty-five miles an hour, while others can drive recklessly at a rate of twenty miles an hour. Common sense clearly tells us that every human being is a distinct and separate individual and that individuality must be acted upon before we can be considered as applying reason to our human relationship. If we say that there is no time to give each individual proper training, it is merely another way of saying that we haven't time to be sensible about affairs that not only concern us, but that have to do with the safety, comfort and happiness not only of the entire population, but of ourselves as individuals.

Of what real value is wealth to the average man or woman if its possession tempts criminals to kidnap their children? If common sense were even reasonably applied many more individuals could attain wealth and none of them would have to bother about the safety of their children and loved ones because of criminals.

Moderation, tolerance, temperance, and clear vision are

necessary for the exercise of common sense, but even more necessary is the courage and determination to take proper action based upon our vision and understanding.

Common sense is a pearl of great price, it carries us safely and harmoniously through our own trials and troubles, but more importantly it enables us to help those who are less fortunate than ourselves in strength of character and determination of spirit.

August, 1934

COURAGE

IT is truly said that the brave man dies but once, but a coward dies a thousand deaths. Courage is not only a vital necessity to obtain happiness, but it is equally important to enable a man to do his work in the world successfully. No one could expect a skilled mechanic to do perfect work when hampered by fear. No one can expect a business man to meet his problems properly when fear walks at his side. Fear is the antithesis of happiness, content, successful endeavor or accomplishment, and, what is far more important, fear is contagious to an alarming extent and spreads to others. Two outstanding examples will serve to illustrate these points. Imagine if you can a board of directors of a corporation, and the mechanics employed in their factory, going about business as usual if they knew that a bomb had been concealed which was scheduled to blow up the entire building within the next hour, the exact time being unknown. We also ask you to imagine some one suddenly rising at a theatrical performance and loudly yelling "Fire" without the contagion of fear being immediately transmitted to a large part of the audience. The disastrous results of panics are largely caused by fear and not by the particular thing that creates the fear. One of the most vital elements of courage is that it is a plastic quality and we can discipline ourselves to courageously speak or act even while fear is predominant in our minds. This attitude, however productive of results, is not conducive to happiness or contentment. In other words a man may force himself to act and speak according to his duties or responsibilities with equanimity and courage and go about them with a calm and certain poise, as a natural thing. Along physical lines many men have learned their lesson. Dangerous work of any nature never lacks for volunteers. Even certain death is unable to deter men from their duties and responsibilities. There is no real lack of physical courage in the world today if the proper motive is produced to bring it forth.

Mental courage, however, is a far rarer attribute of the average individual. It is practically impossible to get a large proportion of human beings to face the facts, to see their duty, accept it, and quietly go about its performance. There is no lack of good judgment among the citizens of our own Country, but this judgment is often wilfully perverted and more often unknowingly affected because of the disposition on the part of even the average intelligent individual to let personal opinions, desires or interests affect his judgment. Mental courage consists largely of deciding as to the wisdom of our speech and action and operates also in self-discipline as regards our thinking processes. Wisdom has to do with permanence and the resources of expediency and opportunism can never be classified as being wise. If a course of action does not yield beneficial and worth while results in the long run, then temporary benefit or result is merely an obstacle that delays a necessary and inevitable change from the path of foolishness to one of wisdom. If a thing is not right and just then it can never be wise, and if mental courage were used universally there would be comparatively little need of stressing moral courage. It is estimated that the human race, even in the most intelligent circles, rarely uses more than two per cent of the intelligence of which it is capable, but even if this be true we would still, by using twice as much intelligence as we do, practically multiply our benefits about ten times. One of the most remarkable aspects of humanity is the contradictory tendencies in a man shown by first congregating with many other people for companionship, safety, comfort and opportunity, and then immediately proceeding to look out for himself and to care little what happens to the others. The spirit of cooperation does not seem to be a natural and automatic part of the average man's mentality. In almost every case the small spark that exists has to be fanned into a flame by some outstanding individual or group in order that it may be made effective. In fact cooperation is usually secured by a promise or hope of individual benefit, whereas cooperation itself is the very thing that creates and makes possible the benefit, and if cooperation were properly exercised such benefits would be received regardless of whether any promises or hopes were held out to those who cooperate. It is the courage to think about things in this manner and to realize that bringing benefits to others will automatically bring an increasing benefit to ourselves that is really needed in the world today. Why should we feel the necessity of battling with our fellow men, for power, glory, position or wealth, when by intelligent cooperation, which really means working together, we can create two or three times as many benefits for everyone concerned instead of a smaller amount apportioned only to the victors in the battle? Everyone loses when we fight, and everyone gains when we cooperate, and mental courage is required in order that we not only recognize this fact but act upon it. The first responsibility comes to the individual and he cannot escape it. If he is not cooperating for mutual benefit with other men or with a group then he should immediately seek an opportunity for so doing, it always being understood that this cooperation must be for a worth while and honorable purpose and the benefits must not be limited to just a few individuals. The strength of cooperation lies in being large enough to achieve beneficial results but not too large so as to be ineffective or unwieldy. Remember then, that mental courage requires thinking with all the wisdom that we possess, seeing the wise course of action unaffected by personal consideration, and immediately and straightforwardly following that course to its conclusion.

Moral courage is of a finer and more delicate quality than either mental courage or physical courage and is therefore more easily set aside or rendered negative by personal feeling, desire or prejudice. Moral courage has to do with distinguishing between right and wrong, between a course of action that is ethical and one that is not, but its chief value is in being able to distinguish the right course of procedure and to follow it regardless of consequences. One vital factor of moral courage is the elimination of inactivity where moral questions are concerned. The large majority of human beings seem to consider that if they refrain from wrongdoing that they are highly moral, without realizing the essential fact that if they also refrain from doing things that should be done that they are thereby to that extent nullifying their own moral standards. It is much easier and sometimes far safer to refrain from action altogether than it is to support and give backing to that which is right and just, and the average individual is content to follow this course. Moral courage has this in common with both mental and physical courage, that the lack of permanent use makes the quality weak and uncertain. The man who asks himself whether a certain course of action is safe or beneficial before he asks himself if it is right and honorable, is sadly lacking in moral courage. Moral courage has to do with justice, honor and ethics and not with safety or benefit. It is also true, however, that the man with moral courage eventually finds himself with far greater benefit and far greater security than those who strive only for personal advantage and personal safety. It can be truly said that no man can be wise unless he is also moral, for the greatest wisdom that has been exemplified through the ages has been brought about by the raising of ethical standards. Without these our physical and mental attainments would have been not only impossible but of very doubtful value if achieved. There is sufficient moral courage within the average individual to guide him properly along honorable paths. The only thing that is needed is desire and a disposition to make use of this quality. This can be implanted by various methods, but probably the most efficient means of turning men's attention in this direction is to enable them to realize that interest in other people's welfare, fair play and square dealing, backed by common sense, will undoubtedly bring them larger reward, benefit, and standing, than any purely selfish course, and, far more, that it will enable them to find a proper amount of real happiness. In mentioning common sense we unhesitatingly state that common sense dictates and demands that men who desire to establish ethical standards and fair play as their code of speech and conduct should organize efficiently with other men of like standards and ambitions. It is not only hard but almost impossible for a man to travel the road of moral courage alone and unaided. It is possible to remove yourself from the every day world where you are assailed by its complications and temptations, but this is impossible for the average man to consider, and, if it were possible, still rather cowardly. It is far better for a man to establish a record of right living of about sixty per cent, under ordinary every day conditions, mingling freely with his fellow men and doing his share of the world's work, than to isolate himself and reach a record of ninety per cent. The world's welfare can never be advanced to any marked degree by those who do not mingle with their fellow men and meet the hardships, temptations and vicissitudes that beset the common run of mankind. The moral courage of American citizens is fully equal to all occasions, but the desire to use this courage must be awakened and strengthened. This does not by any means imply perfect conduct or anything approaching thereto, for we are still human beings and subject to our own weaknesses. It does imply, however, having established standards of right conduct that are practically universally acknowledged, and that we refrain from trying to make our own course of action appear to be right when we know only too well that it is wrong. In other words it means the banishment of hypocrisy, and the willingness to accept proper punishment for any wrongdoing, whether legal or ethical. Moral courage is a weapon that can conquer every obstacle save death, and with its aid even death may be approached without fear or trembling, and accepted with nobility.

September, 1934

JUSTICE

JUSTICE is probably the hardest quality of character to obtain and to steadfastly adhere to. The qualities of honor, loyalty, ambition, pride, and confidence are more or less habit forming, and therefore grow stronger and more dependable as the days and the years go by. Common sense, however, is only partially habit forming and we have to be continually on our guard to see that common sense is used at all times.

Justice is an even more elusive quality than common sense, chiefly due in large measure to a misunderstanding as to what justice really is. Those who cry out most loudly for justice are often those who are most unjust themselves.

The whole field of human behavior is covered by activities on which this quality has a direct or indirect influence. The differences between capital and labor, between the rich and the poor, between master and servant, between all those who are in authority and those who are under their control, must be resolved through the use of this quality of justice.

The differences between husband and wife, parents and children, members of the same family, acquaintances, neighbors, friends, strangers and enemies, must finally be solved through the use of this quality. Differences between nations and groups, between social sets, between organizations and welfare groups, between the different religions and between political parties are conditioned in their solving upon this vital and important element of justice.

In order therefore that we may understand how to apply this quality it is necessary that we understand what it means. It means fair play and a square deal, no more and no less. The people who are willing to give others more than they are entitled to are just as much to blame for hampering and obstructing justice as those who give people less than they are entitled to.

We must clearly distinguish here between outright gifts and rewards. Gifts are made in most cases from the heart and to bring joy and pleasure to both giver and recipient. Rewards should be conditioned upon the value and worth of the results or effort which are rewarded. A workman's wage is his reward for honest endeavor, a child's report card is his reward for the same thing. Promotions of workmen or children in school are additional rewards and must be conditioned upon a satisfactory fulfillment of their obligations. Each worth while effort in life is entitled to a reward of some nature, but it actually must be an effort.

Rewards should never be considered as a substantial recompense for merely being good. It is a man's duty to himself to do that which is right, and he should not be rewarded for doing those things which he should never fail to do. However, when any honest and sincere individual puts forth an effort, even in small measure, to do good for others beside himself then he should be amply rewarded in accordance with the beneficial results obtained for those others. This applies to all phases of life, social, political, religious, and business.

It is equally true, however, that those who do things against the welfare of the public or of individuals should be punished in equal proportion to the damage inflicted. This conception of justice is usually ignored by the majority of individuals. They are not willing to be punished for the unjust things that they do, although they are vociferous in their demand for a reward for the things they do that are just.

Individuals who are "spoiled" by fond parents, affectionate relatives, or generous friends, automatically feel that they should have at all times a better break in the division of desirable things than the average person has. The average parents have no more right to demand more than justice for their children than they have the right to demand more than justice for other people's children, or for anyone else, yet parents who do demand this would be greatly insulted if someone suggested that they be punished for perverting the spirit of justice.

The poor man who looks with disfavor upon the wealthy would certainly not desire to be punished for wasteful and improvident habits, although many workmen thoroughly realize that a considerable number of their fellow workmen spend money on carousing and drinking that should be spent on their own family.

The honest hard-working man who saves a little money gradually and attends to his duties diligently so that in time promotion and a larger income are secured by him, who then buys a home on installments and continues to live an orderly and industrious life, is certainly entitled to the results of his industry, thrift, and sacrifice. The man who is so unjust as to feel that a man of this type should have his home taken away from him in order that the proceeds might be shared with those who have been profligate and personally selfish is not only unjust, but is a traitor to fair play and good sportsmanship.

A large majority of the extremely rich portion of our population use their money in ways that are beneficial to the poor man. The investment of surplus wealth provides jobs for many men who would otherwise be destitute and this is entirely aside from the fact that some of these wealthy individuals may be intolerant, overbearing, cruel or essentially selfish.

The personal traits of the individual are not passed on to his money and the money of a cruel miser, if put in proper channels, is just as able to provide work for men to do as the money of a kind-hearted philanthropist. The great trouble has been that people desire to associate rich men and their money, whereas their wealth is a distinct and separate thing from the individual.

A very rich man may use his wealth in many cases to obstruct justice but this can only be to a limited extent and the beneficial influences of money used in business and trade go far beyond the possibilities of any individual use for personal aggrandizement. To put it practically, the more selfish the wealthy are, the more they will put their money to good use, as by that method they secure greater profits. The mere fact that a small number of individual rich men have been able to put their money to profitable use for limited periods in ways that were not good only emphasizes the fact that permanent profits and increasing profits necessarily depend, so far as ninety per cent of our business men are concerned, upon bringing good results to others.

If we are just, therefore, we can no more criticize the rich man than we can the poor man, and it is not the quality of justice, but the numerical superiority, that causes most individuals to "stick up" for the poor man. The poor man is entitled to absolutely no more justice than the rich man, and the rich man is entitled to no more justice than the poor man, but the question of rich or poor should not enter into consideration. The sympathies of practically all American people are with the poor man, but their personal interests and profits naturally turn their thoughts to money instead of men.

The small merchant in a corner store struggling to make a living does not feel that the poor man should expect him to share what he has accumulated, at such great cost to himself of sacrifice, energy and time. The workman who receives his pay envelope would resent a man who was not working demanding that he share his wages with him.

There is no clearly drawn line between capitalist and poor man. Every man who has any possessions at all is a capitalist to that extent. Justice demands that the question of riches and poverty not be brought into our judgment of an individual, that judgment should be based upon the man's character, abilities, and accomplishments, especially in those activities by which others are benefited.

In marriage relations the question of justice is almost completely ignored. Marriage is a contract as between two people. But as the terms of the contract are not itemized there are comparatively few individuals who live up to it. Certainly one of the conditions of the contract is consideration of the comfort, welfare and happiness of the other party. Automatically therefore, when husband and wife quarrel, when bitter and angry words pass between them, when they lose their temper, when they are grouchy, blue, tearful or cross, they are not only being unjust but they are being dishonorable because of the fact that they are breaking one of the principal terms of the contract. But somehow neither husband nor wife in such cases feel that they should be punished, they seem to feel that what passes between them is their own affair and that it is the business of no one else.

It is everybody's business when anyone breaks a contract. The general public is entitled to know that they are the kind of people who do break a contract, and the general public has a right to punish them in its own way for being that kind of person. In other words when any individual acts in a dishonorable manner the public is entitled to know that such an individual is dishonorable to the extent specified, so that the public can be on their guard against him or her. No man and woman should be able to live what is called "a cat and dog's life" and still be allowed to continue to live together. Justice demands that those who continually disregard other people's rights, comfort and welfare, should be excluded from association with other people until they can learn to regard their responsibilities with proper consideration.

In regard to the law itself we find that justice is represented as blind, this means technically that justice weighs the offense and is not affected by the people concerned. This in fact, however, does not occur, as justice is administered by human beings and often far more consideration is given to the individuals involved than to the facts in the case.

One of the principal obstructions to justice has to do with the political nature of our courts. Judges should be appointed for life and not be under political pressure of any nature. It is hard enough for human beings to pass upon questions that relate to the life, liberty and property of their fellow human beings even when they are unhampered by any restrictions imposed by consideration of their own personal welfare, but it is practically impossible under the present conditions. It is just as important that judges and enforcement officials be properly punished for unjust decisions or persecutions made under pressure of personal, financial or political influence, as it is that they be freed from political punishment when they decide cases according to their honorable and best judgment.

Justice has to be continually striven for and fair play and square dealing have to be at all times uppermost in our thoughts. We can never hope to attain one hundred per cent justice for everyone, but mankind, recognizing our own human failings, would be content with considerably less than perfection.

If human beings knew that they would never be punished for things of which they were innocent, and that they would be reasonably rewarded to some extent for the things they did that were worth while and beneficial to other men, we feel certain that the average man would not only be content but would be practically satisfied. The fear of being unjustly punished is the most vital and important element to eliminate, and the recognition and respect of their neighbors, friends and community, for the things actually accomplished by them as an individual, would give increasing hope, comfort, satisfaction and ambition to the larger part of our citizens.

Let us therefore try to exemplify in our own thought, speech and action the quality of justice, through the simple use of common sense judgment as to fair play and good sportsmanship, not only in our business activities, but in our social activities and in our own homes.

All members of a family, even small children, have their own individual rights and their individual responsibilities. These rights should never be invaded, but on the other hand responsibilities should not be evaded. A child has a right to know why things are right or why they are wrong. Obedience without intelligent understanding may be destructive of a child's strength of character. Emergencies may justify the demand for instant obedience without explanation, but this explanation should be given at the earliest suitable opportunity.

All men or women have certain rights such as, a certain amount of privacy, courtesy, consideration and cooperation, from the other party. These rights cannot be given away, for no one has the right to accept such a gift. If families would treat each other with the same amount of courtesy and consideration that they give their acquaintances, justice would then assume a more important and vital place in the American home.

Justice like charity begins at home and from there it spreads out automatically to all other fields of human behavior. Where personal rights are disregarded in the home we inevitably find that such rights are disregarded elsewhere, and where individuals are willing to disregard other people's rights for the benefit of their home and family we find even a greater degree of injustice in the home itself. We must always remember that those we love can never be entitled to more than justice and that even our enemies are never entitled to less.

October, 1934

Ambition and Pride

AMBITION AND PRIDE are two important elements of character, but it must not be forgotten that these qualities may serve the purposes of both good and evil. These qualities in a man of high character become of invaluable benefit to the world, for the simple reason that Ambition and Pride of the *right kind* are possessed by such a man. A man is not truly ambitious who merely desires to acquire possessions, place and power, but he is truly ambitious if he desires to acquire these through his own abilities and his own efforts without causing harm to other people in the process. It is not even necessary for him to desire to benefit others, for the benefits to other people would automatically accrue through his own success along the proper lines. It is only necessary that he refrain from harming or oppressing other individuals. There are ambitious men in all walks of life, but unfortunately most of them are concerned with their own advancement rather than the benefit that they can confer upon other individuals. This is a rather short-sighted policy and defeats its purpose to a large extent over any lengthy period of time. The politician can last only so long as his constituents really believe that he is sincerely trying to look after their interests. In social life the real leaders of society can last only so long as the members of such society really feel that such leaders really represent them in the way that they want to be represented. When it comes to finance and business the element of leadership seems to be slightly obscure, as the power and prestige of money and business position have a remarkable influence over most human beings. It still is clear, however, that in the long run the financier must prove himself valuable not only to his stockholders, but to the general public which invests its money or deposits its funds with him. In business circles the competent executive has learned that he needs to satisfy his customers as well as his stockholders. However true it may be, in individual instances, that small groups of men profit by the subjugation or exploitation of the general public, it is also true that the business concerns and financial institutions of long life and prosperity have attained their ends through consideration of the desires and needs of the general public and through the permanent endeavor to render the people themselves a real service.

Ambition may truly be said to be a permanent desire to rise to places of importance through a man's own acknowledged abilities in an honorable manner and for an honorable purpose. It is quite true that ambition is to some large extent associated with the acquiring of money and possessions, especially in the beginning of a man's struggles, but it is also true that the really ambitious man merely thinks of these possessions and this money as a means to an end and not the end itself. Most worth while men desire place and power and it is necessary to acquire money and possessions to secure this place and power. It is even true that most ambitious men of good character desire to use this power and position wisely and have no real intention of causing harm to others, with the possible exception of certain business enemies. The real trouble lies in the fact that in a large number of cases a man's ambition secures control of him and causes him to do many things that he would not think of doing if his ambition had been kept in his own control. At such times exploitation becomes a matter of profit-making only, and business trickery and deceit merely a matter of getting ahead of the other fellow. So long as the quality of honor prevails in a man's character there is no danger of his ambition over-reaching itself and bringing him under its control, but the first step in the wrong direction merely makes it easier to take the second and third steps, until finally he finds himself skirting the very edges of the law itself, and sometimes transgressing it. Ambition with honor is a wonderful help and benefit to the community, state and nation if salted with the proper degree of common sense and practicality, while ambition without honor is a dangerous weapon and is likely to injure everyone in its immediate vicinity. Both common sense and honor need to be linked up with ambition in order to make it worth while, and care should always be taken that ambition can measure up to the requirements of both honor and common sense.

Pride is a most valuable and useful trait of character if used in the proper way and for the proper purpose, but this pride should be largely due to the fact that a man is of real service to the world that he lives in and should be something that he keeps in his heart and does not demonstrate offensively to others. It is often said that a man is proud of his own country, but what a man really means is that he loves his country and thinks it a very wonderful place to live in. We can be proud of the attainments of those we love, we may be proud of their possessions, their personality, or their character, but this is not so much a question of pride as it is of appreciation and recognition of worth while things. False pride has to do largely with trying to bask in the halo of others, while real pride has to do with the worth while things that we ourselves have accomplished, with a due feeling of humility that the results have been so meager. Pride of the right type almost inevitably concerns itself with worth while, honorable and noble things that have been accomplished and to our participation therein. No one can truly be said to be proud of being an American unless he show by his action and his attitude that he is the kind of man of which America can be proud. The man who desires to bask in the limelight of citizenship, in a country so glorious as our own, without endeavoring with all his heart to live up to the responsibilities of honor, loyalty, courage and common sense, so wonderfully exemplified by our forefathers, is not really proud in the best sense, for otherwise he could never shine merely in the reflected glow. If he were really sincere he would at least endeavor to do his own small part in helping achieve worth while things for his country. It can be said with a reasonable degree of certainty that you can be proud of the accomplishments of those who are in lower positions in life than yourself, but that you are not in a position to be proud of those who are above you. In other words a man can be proud either in himself or in others only so far as his own attainments permit that privilege. Beyond that point what he calls pride is only a tribute to greatness and a recognition of higher attainments than he himself has been able to reach.

Let us always remember that both pride and ambition in the true sense of the words are limited only to the measure of our own attainment in character and understanding. We cannot be proud of what we do not understand ourselves and to say that we are is a misnomer. Pride is a recognition of attainment and unless we can recognize through our own understanding then we cannot be proud. Ambition is an intelligent desire to build ourselves through benefiting others, and pride is an intelligent appreciation of worth while qualities and attainments. In order to give this intelligent appreciation it is necessary to have arrived at the point where we have exemplified it in our own character. It is impossible to truly recognize something that we have not experienced ourselves.

In order that we may clearly understand true pride we must recognize that there is a false pride. True pride builds up and supplements the good qualities of a man's character. False pride tears down and destroys the usefulness of these same good qualities and accentuates the bad ones. This article has to do with true pride and it is necessary for each individual to understand that he is able to appreciate true pride only to the extent of his own understanding and accomplishments. Pride is a recognition. Recognition means understanding and understanding comes only from experience. There are many things in which different individuals can take pride but regardless of the persons or achievements of which we are proud there must be an understanding within our own hearts and minds and this understanding can only be secured by personal endeavor and achievement. A poor mother, herself uneducated, may so instil certain elements of character into her children that, regardless of the high pinnacle that they may reach, they may always look up to her as the source of their own character and their own attainments. Many of the noblest and most important individuals in the world are the unknown fathers and mothers of those who achieve greatesss in its true sense. These fathers and mothers have not only been able to understand and appreciate the really important things of life but have been able to instil these principles thoroughly in the minds of their own children. This is possibly a greater ability and one much more worth while than any of these children may ever be able to attain. Public acclaim and recognition are not the true elements of greatness, but the ability to live the right kind of a life and to follow principles regardless of consequences is truly a measure of greatness. If in addition to this ability we have the still rarer ability to instil these principles in the minds of our children we can then realize that we have the right to justifiable pride, without regard to our position, place, or importance in the minds of the general public. True pride must come from within the heart for worth while deeds performed and no benefit that we can confer upon humanity will ever be so valuable as to transmit to others through personal example and by helpful guidance the elements of character which go to make up a real man or a real woman.

November, 1934

SELF-CONTROL

SELF-CONTROL is probably one of the most important essentials to a well rounded out character and is absolutely necessary in order to make an individual dependable and reliable. Self-control does not presume a dumb or ox-like attitude of passive acceptance but on the contrary presumes an intelligent appreciation of circumstances, situations, and people, and a further intelligent appreciation of proper thought, speech, or action to such situations.

There are times when a man may be righteously angry but this anger should always be caused by the violation of morals, principles and ethics, and not because of such actions being personally unsatisfactory to himself. All other emotions should be controlled with the same end in view. We have no right to force upon other individuals the burden of our own sorrows, worries, or tragedies, by the means of either speech or action. It is not necessary for us to be gay and happy in the face of personal sorrow such as the loss of a loved one, in fact, it would be inhuman, but on the other hand we should not act in a manner to depress or worry others because of our own grief. In other words we should not be hypocritical and pretend a lack of feeling, but we should be considerate and realize that we should not make others suffer because of our own misfortune.

One of the main evils of liquor drinking is caused by the loss of self-control by the individual who partakes of the liquor. This is evidenced in mild cases by a false exuberance or feeling of well-being and in others by too much, or too loud conversation. The more definite forms, leading to complete drunkenness, are only too well-known. The temperate use of alcohol is probably not actually harmful to the normal individual. Temperance, however, has a relative quality and varies with different individuals. Temperate drinking can be measured by the effect created on the drinker. If he can think, speak and act exactly as he did before partaking of the liquor, then he is drinking temperately, but if there is any appreciable change in his thoughts, speech or actions, then he is drinking intemperately.

We are trying to make this particular distinction because we realize that a considerable number of those who drink do so because of the very reaction, which makes them feel, as they express it, better. Possibly in some cases a man might need liquor as a medicine, in order to take the weight of his burdens and cares from his shoulders for a certain length of time, but the proper thing for him to do under such conditions is to go to bed as any sick man should and then take his medicine. We do not usually favor the practice of medicine in public places and on other people's property. If, however, we are not in the condition of mind or heart where we can classify liquor as necessary medicine then we must admit, unless we are actual topers, that the liquor is consumed for the purpose of making us feel differently from the way we felt before we drank it.

We are not going into the question of conviviality or of livening up a party except to say that these very titles presume a change from the normal to the abnormal and this change is often a source of annoyance, bother and trouble, not only to non-drinkers, but to all those who actually do drink temperately. The real cause for objection on practical grounds has to do with the distorted viewpoint caused by the drinking of liquor beyond the point of temperance. If a man's affairs are in bad shape or if he is undergoing personal suffering or hardship, the last thing in the world that he should do would be to lose his self-control for even a short time. He should by all means avoid drinking himself into a condition, regardless of the quantity of liquor necessary to bring about that condition, where his affairs look better or worse to him than they actually are, or where his suffering and hardship seem less than they actually are.

There is always grave danger, when we face the problems of life, in taking the course which will not in any degree help to solve the problem, but may instead complicate it seriously. Suffering has to be borne like a man in order that a man may really develop his character. It is unthinkable that a man who has lost an individual who is near and dear to him should drown his sorrows in drink, and at last arrive at a point where he has no regret or even memory of the fact that the loved one is lost.

From a business standpoint it is also extremely regrettable that a man who is suffering reverses, should take enough liquor to make him feel that his condition was not as bad as he thought it was. This false feeling of betterment inevitably decreases the perception of necessity for action and the urge to immediately begin to work out of the situation. Most of the derelicts of our cities are men who have turned to liquor instead of to efficient work in the solving of their problems.

We believe that the personal liberty of an individual entitles him to drink liquor if he so desires, but not at the expense of the comfort, content and happiness of others. Practically any individual who has partaken of liquor and is at that time in, or shortly thereafter goes to, public places such as dining rooms, dance floors, streets, or transportation agencies, is obnoxious to many others from the sense of smell alone, even if their conduct and speech are exemplary. One drink of liquor can sometimes make a charming young woman, due to the odor of the liquor on her breath and in her mouth, appear to have been drinking heavily. Sometimes the odor is not particularly noticeable when you are near individuals who have been drinking, but their loud and persistent talking, and the excessive hilarity when there is no humor present, is always obnoxious to quiet and unpretentious individuals.

In drinking, at private parties, whether at home or otherwise, the drinkers are usually obnoxious to those who do not drink. One of the bad habits that drinking induces is the insistence that other people drink also, regardless of their own personal desires. No one has any more right to insist that another person shall drink than they have to insist that they shall not drink, but the real trouble is that drinking people usually forget a part of and sometimes all their consideration for others and their feelings.

Probably the worse social feature of drinking aside from the misery caused by excessive drinking is the loss of courtesy, consideration and even good manners by those who partake too freely. The worse part of the situation is that the individuals are too abnormal at the time to realize their lack of courtesy and consideration, and are equally unable to remember their offenses after they are sober. The proper answer in the application of self-control should be that if a man can drink like a "gentleman" then it is perfectly in order for him to drink up to the point of normality, but if he cannot then he should not drink at all. A man's own opinion is worthless in this regard, but any sober friend or relative of intelligence and good manners can readily supply the answer.

We have devoted a great deal of space to this subject of

drinking liquor as it seems to be so misunderstood. We have carefully avoided discussing this from the moral standpoint, or from the economic point of view, we are referring to it strictly from the standpoint of self-control of his own actions by the individual who claims to be a gentleman, with due consideration for the rights and privileges of other individuals. Those who drink in moderation are probably the greatest sufferers because of the speech or actions of those who drink to excess.

It is impossible to set a standard of measurement for everyone to follow, but the standard of individual reactions to liquor is known to each individual, or it can easily be ascertained, and this should be a standard used by all those who desire to keep control of their own thoughts, speech and actions at all times.

Love and hate are perhaps the two emotions that are hardest to bring under self-control. Practically every individual knows other individuals that he dislikes in some degree, sometimes intensely. Self-control requires that such individuals be treated with courtesy and with all due consideration for their rights and privileges. This does not mean that they should be allowed to force their company upon you, or that it is necessary to engage in conversation with them. It is not even necessary from the standpoint of courtesy to speak to such individuals, but it is necessary to avoid being obtrusively rude and unmannerly in avoiding them, and to see that no underhand action is taken by you to their detriment. People can at least be honorable enemies even if they are unable to have a friendly attitude towards each other.

Love is the greatest and most powerful of the emotions in its influence upon the life of the individual, as well as upon those with whom he is drawn in contact. It is the one emotion that many people seem to feel transcends honor and duty. The actual truth of the matter is that an individual who is willing to barter honor and duty for love is not capable of love in its true conception. A capacity to love is in equal ratio with the capacity to live clean, decent, normal and honorable lives. Many people seem to feel that love is expressed in its highest form by the willingness to die for the loved one, and by being willing to sacrifice anything and everything for the benefit of the other. This type of love is not the romantic love that is so desired by every normal man and woman. It is a perverted, spurious substitute for the real thing.

It is a comparatively easy matter to sacrifice, or to die for a dearly loved one and is usually taken as the easiest way out of the difficulty. To live the right kind of life and to continue struggling and fighting, both practically and morally, for worth while things for those we love is the hard, but magnificently rewarded path for the real man and woman to follow. It is harder to live with another person for a single year and to studiously refrain from anything that invades their own rights, and to as studiously see that they do not invade yours, than it is to lay down your life for them under the stress of emotion.

We find that the loved ones of a family, husbands, wives, sisters, brothers, fathers, mothers and children, are those who are usually picked out by a very great number of individuals to expend their emotions of anger, dissatisfaction, sullenness, ill temper, grouchiness and depressed spirits upon. It is also these dearly loved individuals that hear all the complaints that we make about life in general. Many members of families can be sweet and courteous to everyone but members of their own family. It certainly seems that if we were going to hurt any-one's feelings we should logically choose someone that we did not pretend to like. The only real reason why members of our family, or other loved ones, are chosen for this purpose, is because they are the only ones in the world that will stand for it. There is no other reason whatsoever. Many of us have seen how in the twinkling of an eye a so-called happy married couple indulging in a very heated quarrel can become courteous, considerate and even affectionate when unexpected callers arrive. Self-control would eliminate the necessity or the desire, to use our loved ones as a safety valve for our emotions.

Love should be gauged entirely by the extent to which a person will go to make the loved one happy in an honorable manner. Little things make up the larger part of life and courtesy, tenderness, consideration, affection and a strict regard for the other individual's rights as a human being, are worth far more to the individual and to the world in general than self-sacrifice, or a dramatic gesture, even to the laying down of life itself. Romance of dramatic dimensions is very rare and cannot occur very often in the life of an individual, but the romance of a permanent consideration, tenderness and affection, with an ever-increasing enjoyment and satisfaction from being in love with each other, is the real romance of life. It cannot be attained except through self-control.

Let us save our best selves for those that we love and if we have the courage reveal our worst selves to the public. The public can then at least have a proper conception of the lack of self-control inherent in our nature.

Joy and pleasure are perhaps the only emotions that it is not necessary to hold a tight rein upon. There is so little of them in the world that we are all glad to see any evidences of these emotions in other people regardless of whom they might happen to be. Let us all, therefore, try to bring more joy and pleasure into the lives of those with whom we are brought into contact and especially into the lives of those we love.

December, 1934

SELF-CONTROL

IT is probably true that fear is one of the greatest enemies of self-control that afflicts the human race. Under the inspiration of fear many of the most timid or cowardly individuals may commit acts that the most courageous would shrink from. "Frenzied by fear" is a correct phrasing of the state of mind of such individuals. They are temporarily insane and therefore a great danger to those around them. This represents an extreme phase of fear, but fear has a great influence on the normal individual in many phases of his existence.

Fear breeds distrust, suspicion, antagonism and hatred, and these feelings cannot be eliminated until the fear itself has been eradicated. Fear is what might be considered a useless emotion with the exception of the fear of God, the fear of being dishonorable or unjust, and the fear of ignorance. Fear of God inspires us to lead the right kind of life, it really means reverence for God and not fear, but the word fear is used in recognition of the almighty power that God wields.

Fear of dishonor or injustice inspires us to think deeply and sincerely as to our thoughts, speech and action. Fear of ignorance inspires us to acquire additional knowledge, and probably this additional knowledge that mankind has acquired has been of far greater help to the human race than any material acquisitions. Fear is a disease, but it is one that can be overcome. We, ourselves have to be the physician, no one else can do more than advise or guide us.

Probably the first thing needed to overcome fear is to realize that ninety-nine per cent of our fears are never realized. Usually the calamities and misfortunes that beset us are not those of which we were in fear, but others entirely different. The wise man has said, "A brave man only dies but once, but the coward dies a thousand deaths." The man who carries fear with him has a millstone around his neck that prevents him from doing anything really worth while, either for himself or for others.

It should be pointed out that human beings are more susceptible to mental and to moral fear than they are to physical fear. The man who defies logic in support of prejudiced opinion, and the man who wavers in his decision as between right and wrong, are victims of mental and moral fear and are more to be pitied than the physical coward, for the simple reason that the physical coward would really like to be brave whereas the other two are deliberately stifling wisdom and conscience, and refuse to be enlightened.

There are many things of which a man should be careful, but there are relatively few things of which he should be afraid. It would be carelessness extending to insanity to tackle a tiger single handed, or to obstruct a rapidly moving express train with the idea of proving courage. The greatest generals have shown caution in the face of overwhelming opposition, but they have not shown fear. Caution is a part of wisdom but listening to the voice of fear is the act of a fool. To have self-control we must eliminate fear from our natures as much as possible, but caution is really a part of self-control and offsets impulsive action.

Impatience is probably one of the hardest qualities for

human beings to eliminate as it is world wide, and affects practically all individuals at some time and under some conditions. Impatience is not to be confused with eagerness, for the more a worth while thing is desired and the more eager we are to possess it, the more we are anxious to work and strive for its possession. The longer a thing is waited and worked for the more we appreciate and enjoy its possession when finally achieved, but merely waiting arouses a feeling of resentment and frustration.

In nine cases out of ten, in striving to achieve a worth while object, there is always something more that we can do, some additional work or responsibility that can be assumed in order to bring the desired result nearer. Impatience is almost inevitably associated with waiting, but unfortunately it is seldom associated with working. If we are really desirous of gaining something for our happiness, then we can in practically every case find something more to do that will bring us nearer to our desire. If we are occupied in doing something to forward our purpose, then we have little time for impatience.

The impatient people are those who, temporarily or permanently, are doing nothing to bring about the culmination of their hopes and desires. When people say that they are impatient it means that they have stopped working temporarily and are indulging in self-pity, in other words they are occupied in thinking how hard it is for them to have to wait for what they want. They do not realize that by just that much they are delaying the acquisition of the thing that they are supposed to be working for.

There is practically no case where something cannot be found to do if we are honestly anxious for the attainment of our object. For instance if a man is in love with a charming young woman but there seem to be insuperable obstacles in the path of their happiness he can still proceed to make himself into the kind of man to whom those obstacles will not be insurmountable. If he is not willing to start in to do this, it merely means that he is not so greatly desirious of attaining his objective as he claims. If a thing is worth having it is not only worth working for intelligently and sincerely, but it is worth, if need be, working for until we die.

A few minor obstacles to self-control are embarrassment, surprise, shock, disappointment and horror, as distinguished from fear. These particular emotions, however, we may pass over, not lightly, but with a full realization that the effect of these emotions will be eliminated or minimized when the more important emotions are brought under control.

Another important emotional element is that of jealousy. Jealousy pertains to affairs that affect the heart, and also things that affect our property, possessions, and our place in life. In regard to affairs of the heart it can truly be said that if we really love a person then we cannot do anything to them that will be hurtful or damaging in the long run. The expression of jealousy toward rivalry in love or friendship, in its extreme form, which sometimes leads even to murder, is not because of love, but rather because of the lack of love for the so-called object of our affection. It is an expression of egotism and selfishness.

Those who truly love another individual are most anxious for the happiness of that individual, and if this happiness means the choosing of another mate instead of ourselves, we still find a pleasure in the happiness of the other regardless of its effect upon our own personal hopes or desires. Jealousy of the place, position or possessions of other individuals is usually associated with envy and is also an expression of egotism, pure and simple. The most damaging effect of jealousy is that it can so easily turn to hatred, and no human being can live with hate in his heart and expect to be either happy or contented. Hatred is like a malignant disease eating away our very vitals and in time it will consume its possessor if it is not eradicated.

Displeasure is another emotion that is probably of far greater significance than most people realize, but ninety-nine per cent of its effect is because it is openly demonstrated. There are thousands of things that people do and other thousands that they refrain from doing solely to avoid the openly displayed displeasure of others, especially those whom they love dearly. Many of these things are right and proper and many of them are not, but the essential point is that they should not be done, or not done for this particular reason. Strong men and women should be willing to bear the burden of other's' displeasure, if they are doing things that are right and justified, or if they refrain from doing things that are wrong and unjustified. Conversely, those who do things that are wrong or refrain from doings things that are right, should expect to pay the price therefor.

Another emotion that is akin to displeasure, but worthy of being placed in a separate category of its own is that of annoyance. We are all familiar with the individual who does not often become deeply angry, resentful or displeased, but who is continually annoyed by the most trifling things. Something is always wrong with such a person and many of us have been bored by the generally upset condition of such an individual over nothing.

We have not mentioned the morbid emotions, such as despair, hopelessness, and all emotions that tend towards looking on the dark side of life, for these are psychopathic and should be treated by an expert on mental diseases. It would be impossible to influence the mentality of these individuals toward self-control for the simple reason that the avenue of approach, the brain, is itself sick, and should be treated by a medical practitioner.

Self-control could be summed up from the standpoint of our reactions, in the word "poise" but self-control has a far deeper meaning. Many people have poise who inwardly let their emotions lead them into paths that are uncontrolled by honor or common sense, and sometimes into criminal activities. We should have poise, not as a mask for our emotions, but rather as a mirror to reflect the spirit that is within us, of courage, strength, confidence, calmness and common sense. We cannot hope to achieve this alone. We need companionship and sympathetic encouragement in the attempt, but far more we need the help of the Divine Creator as the source of strength upon which we can always fall back, when our burdens, our temptations, and our afflictions seem almost more than we can successfully combat.

It is too much to expect of human beings that they endeavor to copy the example of divinity, but there is a word that can be used without egotism to express the idea of an individual who has mastered the art of self-control. That word is "noble." Nobility is not too high for human beings to aspire to, and yet it is high enough to set a man apart from his fellow men.

Self-control is the steering wheel of our body, our mind, and our heart, and if we desire to travel the path to nobility it is one of the most essential elements to our success. Let us learn then, the art of self-control, so that when judgment is finally passed upon us we will not have been found lacking in one of the greatest attributes of nobility.

January, 1935

ARTICLE TEN

CONFIDENCE

CONFIDENCE is necessary for agreeable relations with our fellow men. It is also necessary to content and happiness. It is a mutual transaction in its really perfect form. Those who have no confidence in others should not expect others to have confidence in them. This does not mean that confidence is bestowed upon unworthy or dishonest individuals. On the other hand it does not mean that every one is to be suspected of dishonest intentions merely because you do not know them or their background. Confidence requires a general belief in the good intentions and general honesty of other people, but common sense is required in all transactions, with friends as well as with strangers, in order that no harm may be done, regardless of the good or evil intentions of the other party to a transaction. It is the cornerstone of the structure of business activities. Without it, business of the present-day world could not be transacted. It should be safeguarded, however, against those who would use it for the purpose of fraud, and common sense has to determine our course of action along such lines.

Confidence is one of the most important traits of character from the standpoint of securing happiness or of business success. It is impossible for a man to obtain happiness when his heart and mind are filled with suspicion, or distrust. It is also impossible for him to attain business success if he has doubts and misgivings as to the honesty and intentions of all with whom he transacts business. Everyone must trust someone in order to be happy. The more people one can trust the greater the extent of happiness. Everyone must trust someone in order to transact business. The more people one can trust in business the greater the success of that individual will be.

Practically everyone desires that other people have confidence in them, but few realize that this confidence must be gained by having confidence in others. Furthermore, we must also have confidence in ourselves. It is useless to expect that other individuals will have confidence in us if we are in serious doubt as to our own integrity and honesty. Confidence, therefore, must be built up by a personal and sincere effort on the part of the individual to model his life along the road of right thinking, speech, and action, and to adhere consistently and steadfastly to this road. A man cannot be worthy of having confidence reposed in him one day and be unworthy the following day.

Confidence is another virtue that must come from consistent and steady adherence to right principles. This does not mean that any human being can expect to be perfect. It does not mean that they do nothing that is wrong or that they never fail to do the things that are right. It merely means that a man is sincerely, and honestly striving to do the right thing at all times, and that if he makes mistakes in judgment or yields to temptation, that he will openly acknowledge the fact, and try even harder thereafter to measure up to a high standard.

Confidence requires courage, courage to trust ourselves and courage to trust others. All contractual arrangements, from the simplest form of business agreement up to the marriage union itself, are based largely, or in some definite degree, upon confidence in others. Peace of mind, poise, good manners, strength of character, and many other minor traits of character are based upon confidence in ourselves. No one can truly enter into an agreement with justice and fairness to the other parties concerned, unless they are convinced of their own ability to carry out their part of the contract. It is insufficient to merely say that they are unable to do so, and will have to pay whatever penalty is involved. However where contracts and agreements are broken from dire necessity we should always be ready and willing to do all in our power to atone for the breaking of the contract.

Most individuals seem to feel that confidence has to do only, or almost entirely, with matters of money, but when we consider the relations of husband and wife and the confidence that there must be between them for mutual respect, not to mention happiness; when we consider the enormous amount of trouble and time parents spend on their children to teach them that they must not tell falsehoods, you begin to realize that confidence has to do with all our relations with other individuals in any activity of life.

To say that we must have confidence in others does not by any means indicate that we should trust other individuals with money, valuable information, important documents, or anything else that is capable of being misused, or carelessly handled. Trusting people essentially means that you are not suspicious of their motives, but the bestowal of responsibility means that you not only trust their motives, and their intentions, but that you also trust their good judgment, and strength of character. We cannot in other words trust people in the sense of placing responsibility upon them merely because we love them. On the contrary, everyone has to be tested in order that anyone may know that they are capable of bearing the burden of responsibility, regardless of our personal feelings toward them.

An individual might have a ten-year-old boy whom he could trust to be absolutely honorable so far as his childish mind could comprehend honor, but he could not be expected to assume charge of the erection of a mammoth bridge, for example, because of his lack of knowledge, of judgment, and experience. He would have to go out into the world and prove himself along such lines before he could expect to have such responsibility placed in his hands, therefore confidence has nothing to do with love, friendship, acquaintance, or otherwise, these relations merely give us the opportunity to have a greater knowledge of the individual's ability to meet the tests that life has to offer. Therefore, while we should not distrust others, we should take care to see that our business and personal confidence is given only to those who are capable of meeting the tests with which they will be confronted, regardless of whether they are friends or foes.

An honorable enemy is a far better individual for the purpose of our happiness than a dishonorable friend, or loved one. We may trust some people too much, but we should never trust anyone too little.

There are different degrees of confidence that can be given to different individuals, but this must rest solely upon the previous record of the individual in handling such responsibility, especially in the case of those we desire to help, such as our loved ones, personal friends, and valued employes. We should gradually enlarge the scope of this confidence, so that they may broaden and expand their conception of responsibility, and thereby strengthen their characters.

It is not only necessary that we have confidence in ourselves and in others but it is vitally necessary that we have confidence in God, and in His purposes. Many people fail because they limit themselves and their fellow men by so-called human limitations. It is perfectly true that human beings cannot aspire to perfection, but they can aspire to continual betterment, thereby benefiting the world that they live in, as well as themselves. This desire to be better can come only from the Divine Creator. It is not an inherent instinct in man as an animal, or in his thinking processes. It has to do with his heart and his spirit, and his mind can only receive a vague and dim outline of the general purposes of the Creator, and of the natural laws that He has put into effect. If we can only realize the essential fact that God is the giver of all good, and that man himself has been the creator of all evil. In any case we cannot battle evil, which brings unhappiness, and gain a victory for good, which brings at least all the happiness that we do receive, unless we have the strength and support that comes from the very spirit of God Himself that is within us.

The spirit of mankind is really the only thing that differentiates man from the lower animals. Many individuals try to make it appear that man's reasoning power is the main difference between man and animal. This may be true so far as the actual conflict between man and animal is concerned, and reasoning power has helped to subjugate and conquer the brute strength and ferocity of wild animals, but there is no explanation here of the affection existing between a man and his dog, or a man and his horse, for example. In fact there is no explanation from a purely reasoning process, of love or affection in any of its manifestations. Animals have this feeling of affection, even of adoration and it is certainly not arrived at by a reasoning process. It is a thing of the spirit entirely and comes directly from God.

It is important, therefore, that we recognize that any divine traits in human beings, anything that is noble, anything that pertains to love, consideration, kindness and helpfulness, comes directly from the Creator and is not a product of reasoning ability. Our reasoning ability must be used from the standpoint of accepting such well-known facts as real and tangible, and in figuring out how we can make use of love, affection, kindness, and helpfulness for the best interest, and the welfare of mankind as a whole. Food, clothing and shelter are necessary for a man's existence, but existence itself is not worth while unless somewhere there is love, affection, kindness and helpfulness, or the hope for such things.

It often happens that for a certain period of time in the lives of many individuals the world fails to give them these necessary tokens of interest in, and consideration for, their welfare. At such times it is necessary that we be able to turn to the Creator Himself and to feel that He has undoubted love, affection, and kindness for each of His children, and that He is always ready and willing to help in their emergencies.

Confidence in our fellow men can only come through confidence in ourselves, and confidence in ourselves can not possibly be engendered without a feeling of confidence in the Supreme Being who alone gave us power to think, feel, or act.

February, 1935

ENERGY

ENERGY is necessary for full success in our personal lives but especially in business. We use the word energy instead of health as many individuals in reasonably good health do not demonstrate the energy that is necessary to progress, while others in poor health have demonstrated unusual energy of mind and body. A sound mind in a sound body can be attained by the large majority of individuals if they are actually desired by them. No man who desires success should fail to keep himself in good sound physical and mental condition.

Energy has three main definitions in the dictionary: 1. Capacity for work; 2. power, and 3. force. Energy also has three different methods of manifesting itself, physical, mental, and moral. In these attributes it is similar to courage, but in other respects it is of an entirely different character.

Courage is more or less a result, while energy is a personal condition, which may be improved or stimulated, but which might be covered by the simple statement of saying that we are alive. Energy betokens vitality and life. Courage has to do with the things that a person who is alive is called upon to face. Courage enables us to face obstacles. Energy combined with courage enables us to overcome such obstacles.

Physical energy is vitally important and plays a principal part in our lives. Energy automatically indicates activity and movement, but often it can be applied to improper ends, and for unworthy causes, therefore physical energy is not sufficient alone. However, the person who has sufficient physical energy, in other words the person in good health, can often eliminate many of the ills that affect their mind, or their morals.

Many individuals are condemned for immorality and a low mentality because they are physically ill, regardless of surface indications. This by no means is intended to convey the idea that such individuals should not be punished for things which they do that deserve punishment, it merely means that due consideration must be given to a contributory cause of such wrong doing. The idea for example that all criminals are really sick individuals, should in no way mitigate their proper punishment. There should be a definite effort made, however, to restore them to proper condition, so that their future lives would be normal and well balanced. Before we can have any practical effect upon the mental and moral attitude of those who commit crime, or do anything that is wrong wilfully, it is necessary to determine that no physical obstacles stand in the way.

In like manner, but to a very much smaller degree, the normal man and woman should take especial care to see that their own health is kept up to as high a standard as possible, in order that bodily ills might not effect their minds, or their morals. This can be done in the vast majority of cases, but very often those who are ill need the assistance of others who have energy and courage, to enable them to arrive at this point.

In a small number of cases certain physical conditions are seemingly hopeless from the standpoint of permanent cure. In the large majority of such cases, however, the individual concerned, with the help of friends and loved ones, and with the aid of medical science, can succeed in preventing the physical affliction from having an undue effect upon his mind, or his morals.

In the few cases where this object cannot be achieved it then becomes the duty of the loved ones and the friends of such an individual to see that the affliction is minimized as largely as possible by kindness and consideration for the benefit of the individual who is ill, but it is also their duty to see that such individual does not cause harm or suffering to others, regardless of whether that suffering be physical, mental, or of the heart. Those to whom the invalid is near and dear are entitled to bear with the unavoidable annoyances, discomforts and bothers occasioned by the condition, but they should never be transmitted to others, nor should any individuals be allowed by society to wreck their own lives through the continuous caprice, whims and ill-temper of certain afflicted persons. Such individuals should come under the proper care of doctors and nurses until they are at least in condition where they will not embitter and spoil the lives of anyone, regardless of how near and dear they may be.

No individual has any right to make the choice of sacrificing himself, or herself for another person. Their life is not their own to do with as they see fit. They were put here for the purpose of being of service to others, *many* others, and not to concentrate on serving any one individual, except in special cases where their service to one individual enables that individual to be of great benefit to many others. They are thus themselves indirectly benefitting many others.

Energy is like a tool that is given to us for the purpose of creating worth while results in our lives. It is extremely important therefore, that it not be misdirected or applied for unworthy purposes. Therefore, physical energy must be controlled by the brain and the heart, through the use of intelligence and ethics. Misguided physical energy is responsible for many of the evils that afflict human beings. Bullying by the individual, mob violence by groups, and cruel and unworthy oppression of the weak by the strong, whether of individuals, or of nations, are all examples of misdirected energy. These items, however, are spectacular and call themselves to our special attention.

The greatest harm to the individual man or woman, however, does not come from danger, but from the lessening of their activities due to selfish and unworthy motives. Energy that is used for purposes that are inefficient and unproductive is wasted, and forever lost to the world. Laziness is a result of misapplication of physical energy. Efficiency is the antithesis of laziness.

Efficiency requires that each individual put forth his or her energy in the most worth while and productive manner of which they are capable. The workman on the job, the executive in his office, the clerk at his desk, and the boy or girl at school, should put forth their best effort to accomplish a better and a larger result within a given time. Dawdling, stalling, lack of concentration, listlessness, or total lack of interest in productive effort, still remain as some of the greatest obstacles to human progress.

Lack of energy needs personal and medical attention, but misdirected energy needs mental and sometimes spiritual attention. To make a lazy man efficient you must first cure his mind of slothful habits, and it is also necessary that his heart be convinced that he has a duty to the rest of the world that he lives in, far greater than any duty to himself.

Mental energy must not be confused with the mere ability to guide physical energy in the right channels. Mental energy not only has to do with the quality of our brain being alive and active, but it presumes growth and broadening of mind due to experience, observation, and consistently sought after further knowledge, of worthwhile and important elements that affect the welfare, comfort and happiness of human beings. In other words, mental energy is necessary in order that a man may climb higher in business, social, and moral life.

Physical energy manifests itself particularly in acquiring and using up power and force by proper direction of the brain through common sense. Mental energy asserts itself by an ever-expanding and perfecting process. Due to the fact that our mental equipment recognizes the need for betterment, both in physical and mental activities, we find that our brains rely more and more upon ethics and morals as civilization develops. Mental energy asks the questions, "Is it possible?" and "Is it worth while?" Moral energy asks the questions, "Is it right?" "Is it just?" "Is it considerate?" The key to the proper application of mental attainments has to do with the last word in the above question, "considerate." When our brains have considered things thoroughly from the standpoint of desirability and efficiency, it is then necessary for us to give thought and consideration to their effect upon the general welfare of others as well as ourselves, and also upon the permanent effect on their welfare, as compared to a temporary effect that seems desirable.

A good illustration would be that of a physician who failed to think upon the permanent effects that might result from his temporary treating of a patient. Reputable physicians do not give strong drugs or poisons to patients, except in conditions of great emergency. They must consider the well-being of the individual in the future years.

Moral energy must also not be confused with merely the ability to direct our minds along the proper channels. Moral energy is not only predicated upon life and growth, but also upon a consideration for, and interest in, our fellow human beings. Moral energy therefore, as such, is the possession only of those individuals who are themselves trying to live better lives, and who are intensely interested in finding ways and means by which the welfare and happiness of the human race can be brought up to a higher point.

Those who have moral energy are steadily, if at times intermittently, trying to improve their own standards of conduct, but they do not express this through an egotistical and patronizing manner toward the world at large. On the contrary the improvement of their own standards, if actual improvement exists, automatically inclines them to be tolerant of other people's faults and shortcomings, and their effort is mainly directed toward bringing about safer and happier conditions for the people, so that they may gradually be inspired to better their mental and moral state of mind as well as their physical condition and welfare.

Moral energy is needed at this stage of the world's civilization as greatly as at any time in past history. So many startling changes have been made in the structure of the world's society, that many individuals advocate change as a desirable thing in itself. The old order is branded with opprobrious names and designations. There is a constant tendency to say that nations and groups need a new outlook on life. It is rather strange that so many individuals can be persuaded that change in itself is desirable. When change is accomplished by reason of growth, of expansion, of progress, then we should welcome it with open arms, but the uprooting of long established custom and usage brought about through hard experience and the failure of other methods, merely to replace them with some untried and unproved substitute, is worthy of the mentality of a moron.

Honor, consideration, kindness, fairness, and straightforwardness are certainly very old traits of character, but none of us could gain much satisfaction in living in a world from which they had been eliminated. This talk about change, of emergencies justifying dishonorable acts, whether of nations or individuals, is somewhat akin to a request that we have a new set of "ten commandments" to replace the ones by which we have been guided for so long a period. Moral energy, therefore, should be constructed upon proper ways and means of using all of the knowledge and experience acquired by previous generations, to establish what those means shall be, to better the conditions of the people definitely, permanently, and constantly. It is futile to figure that good intentions and the desire for beneficial results are the main factors.

There has never been a time since the foundation of this republic that our leading men and women have not desired to really benefit the people. It is the ways and means by which this benefit could be made real, substantial, and permanent, that is difficult of attainment. Impractical idealists can name one hundred worth while results that are desired and hoped for, but it takes the practical everyday man who is connected with the affairs of the people in their daily lives, to name even one practical method by which *one* of these results might be attained.

Moral energy therefore, is the equivalent of the amount of careful thought that we give to permanent and lasting benefits to the people in general, more than any other one criterion. If we apply ourselves properly in this manner it will be almost inevitable that our own growth and progress along ethical and moral lines will be greater and more productive of that greatest of all human accomplishments, the making of a real gentleman, or a real gentlewoman.

March, 1935

RELIABILITY

THE reliability of a man is gauged to a great extent by the promptness with which he meets all appointments and fulfills all obligations, regardless of the personal inconvenience or hardships encountered. He must learn not to assume obligations or make promises that he cannot fulfill. Obligations or promises must be fulfilled, not because of any reward for fulfillment or punishment for non-fulfillment, but merely because a man's word has been given.

There is no relative importance of obligations. A man who breaks his faith in matters of small moment, can never be depended upon to keep faith in larger matters. Reliability includes as one of its vital phases the full acceptance of necessary responsibility, both in routine matters and in emergencies.

Reliability is a result to be attained through the use of the qualities of honor, loyalty, common sense, courage, justice, ambition and pride, self-control, confidence and energy, practically applied to the business, social and personal lives of individuals. Reliability is a broad word and covers the entire scope of the moral, mental, and physical activities of men. A man cannot be called reliable merely because he is strong physically and capable of meeting physical emergencies, he cannot even be called reliable when his mental abilities are on a par with his physical capacity. He can only be called reliable truthfully when he is properly guided by an ethical code or rules of morals. It is not necessary that he refrain entirely from doing things that are wrong or to omit doing things that are right. To assume perfection is to eliminate the possibility of any human being deserving to be called reliable. In other words reliability, in its essence as well as in its broad implication, is a very human trait, but it is about as high as we can go in the scale of character without approaching the Divine.

Too many people desire to draw a great gulf between practical every-day affairs and things that approach Divinity, whereas in this human work-a-day world we have the whole scale of character from that of degradation up to nobility. Along this scale and in practically every class there will be found a large majority of individuals that are reliable about some things. As we go further up the scale the scope of their reliability is increased, until we arrive at the classification of nobility.

Nobility has to do with strength as well as intention. It requires a strong character to be noble. Reliability also automatically requires strength of character. To be reliable implies that we either have the physical strength to perform our proper duties, or that we have the mental attainment to make up for any deficiency of physical ability. This is what is called a sound mind and a sound body.

Sometimes even the handicap of ill health, which affects both body and mind, may still be overcome by those who have a moral strength of character. Generally speaking, however, any individuals are at a great disadvantage who fail to keep themselves in reasonably good health and they are decidedly in grave danger from the standpoint of character and reliability if they allow their mental health to be undermined. Speaking briefly, a man cannot disassociate from himself either his physical, mental or moral nature. They are all part of the same individual.

This is also true of the thoughts, speech and actions of any man. They are all part of him. A man can no more become moral by restricting himself to ethical activity and speech than a rotten apple can be called sound merely because the rot affects only a small portion. If a man's thoughts are not reasonably decent, wholesome, fair and ethical he is still absolutely unreliable regardless of what his speech and conduct actually show to the world. A reliable man will find his hardest job to be that of controlling his thoughts properly. A mind empty of active interests in life is a breeding ground for unwholesome and unethical thoughts. The only way by which a man can obtain control of his own thought processes is to fill his life with things that are good, wholesome, clean and interesting.

Many people turn to wrong doing merely because doing right seems so uninteresting. Of course such people are shortsighted and rather unintelligent, but it is a basic trait of human nature to turn to things that are interesting and enjoyable and we must never overlook this fact. Those who desire to benefit and help other people should concentrate their attention on good things that are more interesting and more pleasurable than the wrong things that compete with them.

Most men and women prefer companionship that is wholesome, decent and progressive, but if the companionship which they receive from good people is dull and monotonous they will almost invariably turn to things that are interesting, exciting and stimulating and to the companionship that naturally follows. In this particular regard the forces of evil have found a great ally in their battle against the right. They use music and song, laughter and humor, beauty and youth, as a lure to things that vary from thrills to degradation. On the other hand, forces of good have just begun to realize that the same attractions, which are wholesome and normal and worthwhile in themselves, can be used to influence people in the right direction. The Boy Scout movement for example, is the most outstanding effort along this line and has perhaps saved many thousands of boys from becoming criminals.

Reliability therefore, not only has to do with the personal thought, speech and action of the individual as concerns himself, but it has especially to do with his thoughts concerning others and his attitude toward other people and toward life in general. If a man's thoughts prompt him to be fair, kind, considerate and just to all other individuals and if he will then apply himself to an understanding of what is fair, kind, considerate and just he will be well started on the road to being reliable. He cannot be considered reliable, however, until he has this thorough understanding.

Many people consider that giving money to individuals is being kind to them, whereas it may be the most harmful thing in the world for certain particular individuals. To be just is even harder, for justice requires just as much the punishment of the guilty as the protection of the innocent. It is not too much to say that while thoughts are the inspiration of a man's character, speech and action are necessary to translate these thoughts into living things. In other words, if a man thinks of some good that might be accomplished but does nothing about it himself and even refrains from mentioning it to someone who might be able to do something, he is stifling his own moral and mental processes and is stagnating instead of going forward.

It is not desirable for anyone to conclude that being good is a very hard end to attain. With the proper companionship and environment it is easier to be good than to be otherwise. The great trouble has been that most people think of themselves as fighting alone and unaided in their efforts to be good, but they assume ample reinforcements and plenty of companionship in their efforts to be bad. This, however, is also applicable to personal cleanliness. We have to fight a continual personal battle to keep physically clean. Yet this is not used as an excuse for being filthy or dirty. If we desire to be physically clean, we also desire to associate with those who are themselves physically clean, and we purposely keep away from those who are dirty and contaminating.

Just as the effects of cleanliness of the body bring about certain satisfactory pleasurable and beneficial results which are worth while in themselves, and just as this same characteristic throws you with people that are more interesting than the average, so will cleanliness of mind not only make individuals more reliable, but it will also bring certain satisfactory and pleasureable results and, which is still more important, will bring us in contact with the most interesting people in the world, providing we only have the ambition to search for them and to keep up the contacts after they are established.

The one regrettable part of the whole situation is that such interesting people have not found the means or proper method by which to keep in touch with each other and have reasonably close association with resultant pleasure and enjoyment. Therefore many fine people are lonely and often without means of pleasant and happy associations and consequently goodness has come to be associated in the minds of many people with dullness and monotony. If we further withdraw so far as possible from those with unclean physical habits we make ourselves exclusive by just that much. If we further withdraw ourselves from those of unclean minds and morals we thereby become more exclusive and have relegated ourselves to a higher plane of existence. In other words, we have progressed almost to the very top of human society. This classification has nothing to do with wealth, education, or personal characteristics. It has only to do with mental, moral and physical cleanliness. Such people are the class from which spring our greatest men and women and it is also the class which is the most interesting and gets the greatest enjoyment and satisfaction out of life.

It is hard to control our thoughts in the right direction even when our intentions are of the best, because of the personal element so largely entering into our attitude and viewpoint. It is probably for this reason that association with others of like mind would bring such beneficial results. The average man or woman can render a reasonably satisfactory judgment as to right or wrong except where they are personally concerned or where someone they love is concerned, but it is astounding how often good people with good intentions can convince themselves that wrong is right or that right is wrong, where they or their loved ones are concerned. Our thoughts being the motivating force of all of our actions, it can readily be seen why so many so-called good people can do things which almost everyone else can see are wrong, but they themselves feel are right, merely because they have deliberately convinced themselves to that effect because of their personal prejudice, desire or benefit.

The reliable man therefore, must learn to look upon life with a sense of responsibility toward others as well as to himself. He must not only control his actions and his speech but he must control his thoughts. To properly control his thoughts he must establish within them a code of rules and regulations of right and wrong and must decide against himself and his own interests just as readily as he would pass judgment upon others. He must not expect too much from other people but he should insist upon fairness in all his dealings with others. He must be reliable not only in intention but in his ability to decide what reliability really is under given conditions and the strength to carry through after he has so decided. The reliable men of the world are not only the bulwark of their nation's progress and prosperity, but also of its very existence.

The reliable men are the foundation of this Republic and while we all as human beings make mistakes and do things that are wrong, it is the clear, wide road before us of good intentions, supported by common sense application and carried through by our strength of character that will bring us to better conditions and to an established understanding that it is the strong, decent and fair men that are really reliable and that it is to them that the Country should always look for its leadership, management and honorable acceptance of responsibility.

April, 1935

Responsibility

RESPONSIBILITY is the sincere assumption of certain obligations, duties or privileges, whether forced upon us by other people or circumstances, or voluntarily assumed. Responsibility is an undertaking or an agreement to perform certain things. We cannot avoid responsibility except by a refusal to undertake this performance, and where the responsibility is a moral one that should be undertaken by us, we cannot avoid this responsibility even by our refusal to accept it. It is composed as are most elements of character, of three parts, moral, mental and physical. It is also divided into three distinct classifications along other lines. These classifications are, obligations of duty, obligations of privilege, and obligations of necessity.

Under the head of physical responsibilities, the first and chief item is to keep ourselves in proper physical condition, so that we shall have physical strength to accomplish our tasks and to deliver each day a little more than our proper share of work to the world. Physical responsibility is also divided up into a thousand minor classifications having to do not only with the physical, but also with the mental work which we undertake to perform. This enters at once into the realm of mental and moral responsibility, for no one should undertake to perform anything of which they are not physically capable and this thus becomes a mental and moral responsibility, that is, the refusal to make obligations that cannot be performed or that should not be performed. If there is no refusal to perform, then the responsibility must be assumed to have been accepted, except in cases where such open refusal would mean death, disaster or great harm to others, as well as ourselves. This implies, however, the right of the other individual or individuals concerned to transfer these obligations to our own shoulders. Where this right does not exist, then the acceptance of responsibility becomes a matter of judgment as to the best interests of everyone concerned.

Mental responsibility has to do largely with correct thought and speech, but it is impossible for anyone to have correct thoughts, or to think correctly without it immediately bringing him into the sphere of moral responsibility. It is practically impossible to disassociate the mental and moral aspects of thought, for it is the process of thinking that enables moral responsibility to dictate what is actually the right thing to do or say. In other words, correct thinking also means right thinking, or judgment, as to ethical and moral procedure. Nothing can be correct mentally unless it is also right morally. Therefore, in using the term mental responsibility hereafter, it must be clearly understood that moral responsibility is not only included, but is the most vital part of the picture. Mental responsibility as to thought, speech and action is perhaps the greatest responsibility placed upon mankind. A reasonable number of individuals live up to this responsibility, as exemplified by their deeds and actions. A far smaller number live up to it from the standpoint of action and speech, but the number who, in addition, live up to this responsibility from the standpoint of thought, is relatively negligible. Regardless of how good or noble we may strive to be, our thoughts are exceedingly hard to control and the only practical method that has been found to be adaptable to the needs of human beings is to force out unworthy and unwise thoughts by filling the mind with worthy and wise objectives that are so interesting, so enjoyable, and so comprehensive that we have neither the time nor inclination for unworthy and unwise thought.

This does not by any means guarantee that we shall do nothing that is foolish or sinful, for many unwise and wrong deeds are committed merely through lack of thought and not because an individual is consciously centering his mind upon such things. This can be more readily understood in the case of speech for we are all well acquainted with the phrase "thoughtless speech." If, however, we eliminate thoughtless actions and speech from the category altogether, we would still have ample freedom for imperfection, as it is usually in what we term our moments of weakness that we succumb to temptation. We are none of us perfect and none of us can ever hope so to be, but we can strive with all of our might to attain a certain high standard that will render us incapable of doing anything mean, vicious, vile or degrading, and even to keep from thinking thoughts of a similar nature.

Inasmuch as it is in his moment of weakness that the average decent man succumbs to temptation, it will readily be seen that a man needs to build up his strength of character in order to resist temptation even in such moments. Therefore, mental responsibility demands that a man become strong so far as possible physically, but much more from the mental and moral standpoint. Temptation is often disguised in other forms, and therefore, mental responsibility calls upon a man to render judgment. In order to do this he must have common sense and straight methods of thinking. For a man to hesitate in deciding whether an action is right or wrong, shows him to be both weak and lacking in common sense. Things that are right are almost always labeled clearly so that anyone can plainly understand what the right thing to do actually is, and in all cases this is also the wise thing to do. The mere fact that a person has to consider whether an action is right or wrong should place it in the taboo class. It is in this particular field, however, that most of the mistakes of decent people are actually made.

There is a broad classification of action and speech which seems to have very little to do with right or wrong, from the standpoint of morals. The question seems to be only as to the wise or unwise thing to do. Here is one of the greatest responsibilities that we have to face for we as individuals have a moral responsibility to do the thing that is wise and we have the further moral responsibility of deciding the thing that is wise to do, not from the standpoint of expediency or temporary benefit, but from the standpoint of the welfare of all worthy persons and of the world in general.

Everyone knows for example, that no one should have to suffer the shame and ignominy of accepting charity, and that each human being should have an opportunity to work for his or her living and to support themselves and retain their independence, regardless of their own personal desires, yet those of us who are able to do so continually contribute to purposes of charity. This does not mean that these contributions should be stopped, however small they may be, for this happens to be the only available method under the present system by which those who are unfortunate can be saved from starvation, disease or death, but it does mean that we have a moral responsibility, as well as a mental responsibility and an economic responsibility, to think about the problem, to cooperate with each other and to gradually take action that will remove the word charity in its now accepted sense from general use.

One particular responsibility we have under the heading of

common sense is to refrain from equivocating, arguing or trying to persuade ourselves that certain wrong things are right, or that certain foolish things are wise, merely because of our own desires in the matter, or because of some selfish purpose, even if it is masked in the disguise of a benefit to someone we love. Those who are willing to do wrong or unwise things for the benefit of loved ones, can be certain that they will suffer the penalty therefor themselves, but they can be doubly certain that those whom they desire to benefit, will also suffer because of their unwise and incorrect actions.

Parents can be too lenient, as well as too strict with their children, but there is always the responsibility of letting children know a right or wise reason for the parent's leniency or strictness. This safeguards a child far more than parents usually realize, for the average mother and father are usually trying to do the right thing by their children and if the children realize this, they will automatically overlook mistakes and errors of judgment made by their parents and respect them for their good intentions. This has another highly desirable effect and that is, if parents had to give a good and wise reason for things in teaching and training their children, it would often force them to refrain from doing certain things, and to go out of their way to do others, as it is practically impossible for a decent human being to even attempt to explain to a child that wrong is right, or that foolishness is wisdom. Hasty and ill considered speech and action by parents to their children should be apologized for and explained even more so than to a grown person, for an adult may understand the cause of such ill considered action or speech without explanation, but a child can often see only the results without understanding the reason.

We have a mental responsibility in business, in society, in politics, and in all matters that affect the welfare of the human race. We cannot avoid or evade this reponsibility by trying to load it upon some other person's shoulders. On the other hand we have no right to accept the responsibilities of another person that should be borne by themselves, without first having done all in our power to see that the other person was put into a position physically, mentally and morally to shoulder their own burden. The giving of money is very often an excuse to evade the responsibility of helping someone to get on their feet through their own efforts. It is true that there is a no more thankless job than trying to resurrect the independence, the spirit or the good impulses of individuals who have evaded their obligations and in some cases forgotten that they ever existed, but we must remember that the world is composed of individual human beings and that everyone of these individuals in some respects must be treated as entirely separate and distinct from all the other individuals in the world. We must have a system by which, like scientists in a laboratory, we can examine such individuals as become necessary to correct and locate the means by which their instincts of good, of pride and of ambition, can be appealed to in such manner as to procure the proper result.

The herding of human beings together in penitentiaries has not produced the proper results, as we well know. The teaching and training received by children in school and college have likewise not produced the proper results in laying the foundation of real character. Governmental and political activities have produced some results but these have been very meager. Religious training has been battling to provide a foundation in character for all our people, but the unfortunate part of this endeavor is that so many people stay away from church or religious activities altogether and others who go to church fail to live up to the principles and ideals which they hear expounded. This leaves in a general way only two avenues that are open to building character. One is the business world. Here, if the individual is fortunate his character will be built up and made stronger and more reliable by the practical every-day needs of his association. Unfortunately a small proportion of the business world is engaged in sharp practices and dishonorable, if not dishonest, dealings. Those who through mischance get into this particular category of business usually have their characters affected adversely and themselves become a problem to the community or to the nation.

The cooperation of honest and reliable business men to set up and maintain a code of ethics is one of their major responsibilities. It is their further responsibility to see that the law breakers and the conscienceless individuals are weeded out.

The other avenue is our high courts of law, especially the Supreme Court of the United States. These courts have the respect and the good will of practically all right thinking citizens, but we must always remember that they must decide upon the questions of law, and not upon questions of honor, which are not always the same thing.

In the final analysis, therefore, just as the individual is entitled to receive consideration from the rest of the world as an individual, so he must accept his physical, mental and moral responsibilities as an individual and not attempt to evade them or to shift them to the shoulders of another person or group.

May, 1935

REASON

REASON can be more or less adequately described as the ability to think clearly and connectedly. The power of reasoning has been exclusively bestowed upon mankind and due to this gift, mankind has been given the responsibility of governing and managing this world that we live in. It can truly be said that reason is capable of surmounting all obstacles in the course of time. The chief danger to reason does not come from outside causes, such as brute strength, great calamities, or the laws of nature. Instead, this danger comes from a perverted method of reason due to unbalanced minds. We are not speaking of insanity in this connection, but of the ability to think, but not the requisite ability to think clearly and in a rational manner. There is a great difference between intellectuality and intelligence. Many persons of great intellect can think through and solve very intricate problems, but have not the intelligence to balance these with the rest of the world's problems so that they assume their proper proportions.

Reasoning implies the acceptance of facts, of knowledge previously gained, of information available, but it also entails the responsibility of drawing proper conclusions therefrom. Sometimes reason is so closely linked to faith that there is no clear cut division between them, but this faith becomes almost a part of the reasoning process. For instance, who can contemplate the marvelous structure of the human body, the structure of animal, bird, fish and plant life without recognizing the essential existence of a Creator so far above our mental conception that He is entitled to our homage, adoration and loyalty.

The mere gift of the five senses is sufficient to establish that divine power beyond all doubt, but there is a stronger and more mysterious emotion that springs from the heart, which has impelled all mankind from the very beginning to reach out for something which we cannot comprehend with these senses, but which we feel is an essential part of the structure of life. The outward evidences of this reaching out of mankind are found in the various religious bodies and religions they profess, which, regardless of the state of civilization, are found in every part of the earth. Even we poor human beings can continue to have faith in other human beings long after so-called facts have proved such faith unfounded. How is it possible then for reason to fail to be a very foundation stone of faith? Does not all of our knowledge and experience show that mankind desires, needs and has to have things beyond the reach of our five senses?

Love is one of the most beautiful things in the world and yet it partakes of the divine. When we say divine we mean something that is beyond the reach of our five senses and yet not beyond the reach of a dim but definite understanding. A young man in love surrounds the object of his adoration with the beauty and desirability that is not at all discernible to many others whose senses are in equally functioning condition. The eyes of love look upon us with sympathy, understanding and tolerance and who can say that these are not directly a gift from the Divine Creator. These emotions are not man made.

The tigress will fight for the life of her cubs. We cannot call this reason, so we call it instinct. Nature's law is that of self-preservation, but the tigress ignores this for a deeper and more fundamental law that was instilled, not by mankind's reasoning powers, but by the Creator's gift of the protective instinct. Many individuals will venture far more in the protection of others who are near and dear to them than in protecting themselves. This does not come from reasoning power, but our reason compels us to admit it as a fact. Reason, therefore, is not only the foundation stone of an active and worth while existence but it is also the foundation stone of our belief in God, of Heaven, of a hereafter. To think that some of our own puny intellects would seek to eliminate a Creator with a powerful and wonderful plan to cover our lives and our future existence is to make traitorous use of the very gifts bestowed upon us by such a Creator.

When we proceed to reasoning along practical lines it is often hard to think deeply and clearly enough to reach the fundamental basis of facts and actual knowledge, but once we let emotion enter into our reasoning processes we instinctively make a mirror out of our perspective and instead of seeing the light of reason and the broad expanse of experience, we usually see only the things that we desire to find, and even the most outstanding warning signals are perverted and distorted so as to coincide with our emotional reactions.

Emotion has its proper and recognized place in the human mind and by this it is of course understood we mean the best emotions, the emotions that are good. The thing that most people fail to understand is that emotion should not play any part in our reasoning processes. Emotion should be a spur to our sluggish thoughts and should impel us to think things out clearly and thoroughly, but once emotion gains control of the thinking process there is no method by which thinking can be made beneficial either to ourselves or to the world we live in.

A good example is a young man in love; he may be swayed by the deepest emotions but unless he cares enough to sit down and calmly work out a method by which he can marry and support his wife and himself with decency and self-respect and independence, then he is doomed to failure as a husband and as a citizen until he changes his viewpoint toward life. Bear in mind that we are not speaking about supporting his family in comfort or in luxury, the amount of money needed does not enter into consideration. It merely means that he assumes the obligation of marriage fully and sincerely and that whatever hardships, struggles and sacrifices may result, he will meet them with courage and fortitude. Just so, emotions may inspire us to do fine and wonderful things, but when we actually do those things, or when we attempt to figure out a way to do them, we must be calm, cool and clear-headed. This does not by any means remove the spirit of enthusiasm from our efforts. Once a man is able to figure out that a thing can be done, then he can let his enthusiasm have full sway in the work necessary to accomplish his object.

Emotions should be the inspirers of effort, and emotions should greatly enter into our actual work in pursuing those efforts, but emotions have no place in the clear and studied planning of the means by which our work will be able to produce the hoped-for results. A large part of the trouble with the world today is emotional and enthusiastic thinking, leaving entirely to other people the actual work. It also seems that the most enthusiastic thinkers, those who claim to be thinking for the welfare of humanity, are almost always those who have had no experience whatever in the lines of work that are needed to produce Utopian results. Some of the greatest crimes against humanity have been committed under the guise of looking after the welfare of the people. There can never be too much real thinking, but there can be an enormous and stagnating surplus of emotional thinking, which is really not thinking at all, but a childish and inane desire to force other people, more worthy and capable than the thinker, to do things that he himself is incapable of accomplishing.

Reason must first of all take into consideration demonstrated facts that have been developed by the experience of mankind. Some of these facts are pleasant to contemplate and some are decidedly unpleasant. But if we desire, even with the worthiest motives, to change these facts into other facts that are more pleasant, it is still vitally necessary to understand the facts that we desire to change. It is not always possible for those who are in a position of power or authority to understand completely the facts concerning various problems, but it is possible for them to select those who have the requisite understanding. This understanding can come from only one authentic source, and that source is actual experience.

Theories advanced without having practical experience as a foundation cannot even be considered real thought, and certainly is not reason. The faculty of reason consists largely of adapting worth while theories to the individual needs and practical benefits of the people and their activities. We doubt if any real authority on finance ever existed that did not base his conclusions upon practical experience; in other words, facts. Many people have what seem to them wonderful ideas and theories for the benefit of mankind, but practically none of them desire to prove this theory by practical application by themselves in a small way. Many of them are perfectly willing to take the responsibility of putting such theories into practice in a large way, for the simple reason that this makes it automatically devolve upon others to do the work connected with applying the theory. Book learning is of great value when built upon the foundation of actual experience, but book learning alone is usually a snare and a delusion. A college professor might conceivably evolve a paper system of handling men, but if he tried to apply this system personally he would make an abject failure because of lack of practical experience. Many individuals have thought out what they considered a perfect system of government, but these individuals, almost inevitably, are persons who have never had any real dealings with government or with human nature. The only people who are fitted to write or talk intelligently in regard to the nation's problems are those who have had actual experience in the solving of such problems. Reason does not demand that we forsake the idea of an Utopia, but it does demand that it be a real Utopia and not a visionary hope. The only Utopia worthy of the name would have as its principal benefit the freedom of the individual. Any scheme which necessitates government being the master and not the servant of the people is not progress, but a reversion to barbarism.

In our personal lives reason must always enter in to protect us not only from wrong thinking but from emotional thinking. The personal viewpoint, interest, or desire is the one great obstruction to, and enemy of, reason. Once we begin to think of how we can prove that what we desire is right, and thereby try to justify ourselves in our own thoughts and actions, we are on the wrong track. We should think of what the right thing to do would be in the case of others who might ask our advice, others in whom we had no interest except the giving of sound and ethical advice. Clear thinking, however, not only requires us to eliminate self-interest or a personal viewpoint from our thinking processes, but it also requires the elimination of advice or counsel from anyone who is not also a clear thinker. The average man usually goes to his friends or loved ones when he is faced with a problem about which he, himself, is uncertain. Sometimes this very friendship or love may affect the advice of the other individual. Advice, therefore, should never be requested, and, if given, should not be heeded, unless the one who gives such advice is the type of individual who will think clearly and with reason, and will then give you the true results of his thinking, regardless of whether you are a friend, acquaintance or stranger. Reason does not demand that we should at all times be perfect, but it does demand that we accept our own faults and failings as such, that we recognize our own weaknesses and shortcomings, and that, incidentally, we do our best to correct them.

Reason is a comprehension of all the good things of life, as well as the bad. Without reason we cannot understand and appreciate the good, the noble, the worth while and the beneficial, and neither can we so easily avoid the evil and the harmful. Reason, therefore, partakes in itself not only of the practical and beneficial, but also of those qualities such as honor, loyalty, justice, courage, etc., that go to make up the real American gentleman. Reason is the staff that helps us along the road, not only to worth while living, but to happiness and to the sure reward of a good work well done.

June, 1935

INDEPENDENCE

IT is most desirable at this particular time, just prior to the celebration of Independence Day, to call attention to the real meaning of independence. Many people even in our own country seem to feel that Independence Day is celebrated entirely because this nation freed itself from domination by any other country, and many other individuals attach to the word independence only the attribute of financial security. As a matter of actual fact independence means freedom. Freedom from support or government by others. This means essentially that America is a self-governed nation, that the real rulers are the people themselves, and that the temporary elected officials are their servants, employed to carry out the will of the real rulers, the people. In other words using the immortal phrase of Abraham Lincoln, it is a "government of the people, by the people, for the people."

The Constitution of the United States begins with the words, "We, the people." It was on this basis that our glorious republic was founded and it has been on this basis that it has grown and prospered. It must inevitably be on the same basis that the nation shall go onward and upward to a higher and worthier destiny. The noble and magnetic attraction of freedom has drawn people from every nation on earth to participate in its advantages and benefits, but far more to participate in the spirit and soul of freedom itself.

It is true that we have made many mistakes in our struggles toward perfecting the mechanism of independence. Many rich men have at various times exploited those less fortunate than themselves, by virtue of their power or their cleverness. Many poor people have exploited the general public by throwing themselves upon the public as a burden. Broadly speaking, however, from the ranks of the honest and reliable day laborer up to the self-made captain of industry there has been an unanimous general process of thought in the minds of American citizens. To all of these men were available opportunities of education, work and acceptance of responsibility. Our nation's record shows that the large majority of successful men have originated from the ranks of the relatively poor. Our history is filled with examples of such progress. Our educational system, while not perfect, has always been available for those who were eager to acquire knowledge. Our business opportunities have always been open for those who were sincerely in earnest in their efforts to make themselves worthy of higher responsibility. Our failure to properly handle one responsibility conscientiously has been a dominant characteristic. Although our nation's existence and our personal freedom depends upon the intelligent handling of our franchise at the polls, it still takes almost a national crisis to get as much as eighty per cent of our voting population to actually take part in the selection of their public servants.

The thought that we desire particularly to bring out in celebrating our national anniversary is that independence can only be secured and made safe by the acceptance of responsibility on the part of the people. We do not select officials to tell us what to do, but we select officials to do what we tell them to do.

If they fail to follow our instructions we have the power to remove them from office. However, when the people, themselves, will not even bother to find out what they do want, it is perfectly natural that politicians will conjure up schemes of their own to offer the people as bait for their votes. This gives rise to concerted pressure by determined minorities and accounts for the great influence that small but well organized groups can exert, not only upon our legislatures, but upon our executive officials. It has almost become a truism that our elected public servants do not consider themselves as the representatives of the people, but on the other hand consider themselves as the representatives of a party, or a political machine. The politicians of the party or the machine are the ones who give the orders, many times irrespective of the desires or the welfare of the general public.

Party platforms have to a certain extent become meaningless as all parties have tried to tempt the people with the same kind of bait. Unfortunately, however, party principles as expressed in a platform have recently been made meaningless in another sense and that is by calm and casual repudiation. This has a far more vital and deeper significance than previous duplications of promises by the two large political parties. If the standard bearers of a party cannot even be counted on to attempt to live up to the party platform, then the premises upon which our elections have been based are struck down, and there is no method by which anyone can figure out what elected officials will do with the authority that is given to them.

The only means by which this can be remedied is for each community to start correcting the situation at home. Their local representatives are the ones who vote for the representatives above them and these representatives should have the will of the people clearly indicated to them before election. This will of the people should apply to candidates for both of the large political parties so that regardless of which candidate is elected, they will be bound to obey the will of the people on the major and most important items. If they do not select representatives that will also obey the will of the people then they can be retired to oblivion. This necessitates, however, that the desires of the people be made known to their representatives, and this requires the sound opinion of men of good judgment and honorable character, who are in no way connected with political machines. Just so long as the people are willing to accept what politicians hand out to them and indorse this hand-out as their own free expression of opinion and judgment, just so long will the politicians be able to control platforms and policies for their own convenience and self interest. The people must not only know what they desire, but it must also be just, fair and honorable. No one class or group should expect special privileges for themselves that are not granted to all other citizens.

There has been an ever growing tendency for a number of years for the federal and state governments to use income tax as a means of securing revenue. This means in drastic terms that the government, itself, depends upon the rich to sustain it. This is certainly getting far away from indepedence. Instead of every able-bodied man contributing his proportionate share of running the government of his state and country, he pays far more in the long run through increased prices if he happens to be poor, without getting any credit whatever for his share in the support of his own government. The rich men find ways and means of making more money so that even after their taxes are paid they still have an enormous amount left. There is no possibility of taking money away from the rich with the estimable purpose of relieving the poor of a burden without making the poor pay much more heavily in other ways. Money that is taken from the rich man by the government is used for unproductive purposes. If the money were left in the rich man's possession it would be used for productive purposes, giving more employment, more wages, and more purchasing power to the average man. If anyone will follow the history of the income tax it will readily be noted that government expenses have risen rapidly and alarmingly as the possibilities of this source of revenue became more apparent. Until the income tax went into effect the annual federal budget was around One Billion Dollars per year or less. All we have to do is to look at it now to see the comparison. There is an old saying that "the power to tax is the power to destroy," and this is only too true in certain instances. It is not true, however, with regard to an intelligent and liberty-loving people, for such peoples will never consent to their own destruction or the destruction of their liberties. They may be patient and long suffering but they will eventually sweep out of office and power those who would enslave or destroy them. It is high time that a limitation was placed by the people, themselves, in a constitutional manner upon taxation. The people are the rulers of this counry and as such have the right and the moral duty to surround the authority that is given by them to their representatives with such restrictions as to make it impossible for their temporary servants to encroach upon their liberties or their possessions.

In view of the growing size of national budgets in all the civilized countries and especially in America, this problem must necessarily be solved or finally government will cost more than the people themselves are able to make. There is no time or space to go into this matter fully, but in a general way the people, themselves, must specify in federal, state and local affairs, just what their legal representatives have the power to do and that any further extension of such powers would be void and of no effect. Witness the controversy that is now going on in regard to the taxing power and the authority over commerce.

Unquestionably, our forefathers who founded this republic

desired a central government for the purpose of protection and of progress. The mere idea, however, that the Federal Government should act in any other manner than as the representative of the states would have nullified all attempts to set up the federal union. The central government was organized solely for the purpose of affording protection against enemies, of handling foreign affairs, and of handling controversies or difficulties as between the states, themselves. It was a union of independent states composed of independent citizens and was specifically modeled so that the central government could never be strong enough to oppress and subdue the states and the people themselves. Individual and personal rights are a natural accompaniment of states rights and when we destroy the rights of the independent states we have by such methods automatically destroyed the rights of the individual. What we need for independence is not more federal authority but far, far less. This means, however, that the individual states and their citizens must accept their own obligations more seriously than in the past. It would be far preferable for certain rich states to lend the federal government money in emergencies than it would be for the federal government at any time to give or lend money to the states. The power to tax may be the power to destroy, but the power to adminster funds or to lend money is also a power to control the people to whom such money is lent, or given. It should not be possible for a federal political party to have such power in its possession.

The states are the possessors, through their citizens, of the entire wealth of the country. When they allow the federal government to take such part of this wealth as is needed for the economic handling of purely federal business, that is just and fair, but when they allow the federal government to possess itself of their resources and then to turn around and lend, or give it back to them with conditions attached thereto, which in a degree places the control of their state and its citizens and their welfare under the central government, they are thus being forced to contribute to their own enslavement as well as to the consequent enslavement of the people.

The war of the revolution gained us our original independence, but, make no mistake, we have had to continually fight for this independence down through the years. There was never a time when it was more in danger than at present, due to the determined attempt to foist so-called reforms upon the people. Most of these reforms are projected and proposed for the sole purpose of securing the votes of the people as a reward for their initiation, it being inevitably certain that these reforms will fall by the wayside and prove unworkable. This is so principally because none of them are founded upon work and upon a man being paid according to his ability and industry.

The gospel of pay without work should be excluded from any future system and the gospel of work for everybody, according to their capacity, should be substituted. Work should be the foundation, and not idleness. Every American adult, except the violently insane and those who are in the last stages of hospitalization, should be able to do sufficient work for which they are fitted, to at least pay for their upkeep and comfortable existence. It is by this means only that we can make and keep Americans free and independent.

It would not be fitting to close this article without referring to an independence of even a higher and nobler type, the independence of the soul and of the heart, which is achieved by having a conscience free from the stain of doing things that are mean, vile, cruel, or inconsiderate of humanity. Also a heart that desires to do at least a little something for those who are less fortunate than ourselves, of helping our country, our state and our community in some manner, and in some degree to be an example to the rest of mankind.

We have a duty and obligation to our country, our state and our community, but we also have a more supreme obligation, although of a different character, to God, to humanity and to our own self respect. These obligations round out our American citizenship, and make the individual citizen not only free, courageous and strong, but also in the fullest meaning of the word independent.

Independence is a treasure to be purchased by our most earnest and intelligent effort, to be fought for at all costs and under all conditions, to never be abandoned so long as the breath of life remains within us, and even after death to be made safe and permanent by entrusting its care to our children and bequeathing to them the intelligence, courage, and strength of character to guard it safely, and to preserve it at all hazards.

July, 1935

SELF-RESPECT

THE dictionary defines self-respect as proper regard for one's own person and character; commendable self-esteem. In spite of this very clear definition of the meaning of this term, and in spite of the general understanding of what the word means, the detailed understanding and application of self-respect to our personal lives is in many cases nebulous and uncertain. It is capable of being interpreted according to the intelligence and ethical attainments of the interpreter. A proper regard for the person demands cleanliness of body, and a proper regard for character, means cleanliness of mind and heart. Our bodies and our minds should both be kept in a wholesome and healthy condition, and this can be attained only by doing our share of the work of the world with as much efficiency as possible, by striving to acquire greater knowledge and efficiency and by successfully combating most of the temptations that yielding to would weaken or degrade us.

Self-respect has nothing to do with what other people think of us or our actions, but it has a great deal to do with being and acting as a fine and noble person should, so that a person that has the proper amount of self-respect must inevitably, except in isolated cases of injustice, also have the respect and esteem of his fellow men. It should be distinctly realized, however, that the motive behind ethical conduct is to satisfy an inner urge within a man himself which prompts him to do the right thing regardless of consequences, and that the motive must never be the desire to gain the plaudits and honors of the world.

Certainly there is nothing that is any way undesirable about a man desiring and trying to attain the esteem and gratitude and appreciation of his fellow men for worthy things that he may accomplish. It is merely desired to call attention to the fact that this particular incentive has nothing to do with self-respect, for occasionally self-respect requires that you do certain things that will bring down on your head accusations and blame, resentment and ridicule, and often this comes from friends as well as foes.

Self-respect must be an inherent part of our character and be used as a lubricant to aid and assist the other qualities of character to perform their functions with a reasonable degree of ease and efficiency. Self-respect is so capable and strong, if properly imbedded in our characters, that we can lean on it when all other aids seem to fail us. A man may be in the depths of despair, he may feel that the world is all wrong, or that it is arrayed against him, but his self-respect will not only prompt him, but will actually give him the courage to carry on like a man, to overcome the obstacles that confront him in pursuing the right course, or at least to die in the attempt, with his honor and his name unsullied.

Self-respect is somewhat analogous in a real man, to the cement with which stone walls are joined together. The cement when properly set will prove to be stronger than the stone wall itself. This is principally because self-respect partakes in different degrees of practically all of the noble and fine qualities of character. It is the guardian of our thoughts, speech and actions, ever present and ready to be called upon. Honor will sometimes seem to be dim and distorted. Loyalty will occasionally become vague and uncertain. Common sense will often desert us under the stress of emotion. Courage, justice and confidence, will sometimes flee away right at the time they are most needed, but self-respect is always on the job, needing only to be called upon to perform its function of protection or salvation. Self-respect never deserts us and we can only avoid its aid by deserting self-respect.

Self-respect evidences itself through thought, speech and action. The self-respecting man will not commit acts that are mean, vicious, vile or degrading. He will not intentionally do things that are cruel and unkind or inconsiderate of other people's rights. Physically he will keep himself clean and free from disease or afflictions that can be avoided.

He will respect womankind, because women are the mothers of the race, with all that implies in suffering, anguish and sorrow, as well as love. This love brings to women such happiness as they receive from life, but it also brings misery when their men fail in character and especially in self-respect. A man who has self-respect in a fair measure has automatically enough of the other noble qualities to satisfy the need that is inherent in all women to have their men the type that they can both love and respect. This applies whether it be father, or son, husband or other loved one. Therefore, the man who claims to have self-respect can never fail to respect womankind in general and to fully realize that a large part of the sins or transgressions, errors or mistakes of women are due to men's influence over them in the wrong direction. Self-respect should impel a man to protect women and not to be unkind, inconsiderate or selfish. Incidentally it may very well be said at this point that self-respect should also keep a man from being the type that can be wound around a woman's finger, as the old expression goes. It means courage and strength to keep from doing the wrong things that women might desire you to do, as well as the wrong things that you might desire to do yourself.

Self-respect should also impel men to be especially kind to children and to those who are unfortunate in regard to health and mentality. This does not mean, however, that we should do too much, any more than that we should do too little, to aid those weaker than ourselves. We should only do what is necessary to awaken their spirit and their desire to solve their own problems, but we should never take these problems upon our own shoulders, thereby causing them to become weaker and more dependent than ever. It is never worthwhile to help a man by giving him money or charity and taking away permanently his independence and self-respect. Charity should never be considered as anything but an emergency aid outfit to be used only until such time as the patient can be taken to the hospital and have the real care and attention that is necessary. This care and attention means restoring the spirit and the morale of the individual. If this is not done it is comparatively true, with all humane consideration for mankind, that the patient might just as well be dead. The person without spirit, morale, independence or purpose in life, has no real reason for existence, but fortunately only one person out of a thousand is the type that cannot have the spirit and purpose instilled into them. Our own self-respect demands that we use our money, our energies and our time to make less fortunate individuals independent of our money as well as of any other money that they do not earn.

In the realm of speech, which also includes written matter, self-respect demands that we refrain from untruth and perversions of the truth, as well as vulgarity and indecency. Language was invented to express the meanings that were given to the words in the language. Self-respect demands clear and honest opinions or statements of facts. People with self-respect do not use words to conceal their meanings, or to pretend to have a different meaning from the actual one, but to reveal their meanings. That is why politics has obtained such a bad reputation in all countries and at all times. Politicians endeavor to distort and make blame-worthy the motives of their opponents and to praise their own motives to the skies. In distorting truth in order to achieve the result of having people believe things different from the truth, they thereby automatically lose their own self-respect.

A man's thoughts should be kept clean and wholesome and the safest and best way to achieve this result is to fill his mind full of worthwhile and interesting material. This can most easily be done by furnishing men opportunities to acquire additional knowledge and broaden their responsibilities, which automatically builds up within them this fine trait of character, self-respect.

August, 1935

STRENGTH

STRENGTH is one of the most essential elements of human character. Strength, however, consists of three classifications; physical, mental and moral, and undue emphasis should never be laid upon physical strength alone. It is important that bodily health be given vital consideration, but if a man's mental and moral equipment has been developed, it matters little as to his size, weight, or muscular development.

Mental strength is important and can be of great benefit to the individual and to humanity if exercised properly, but in order that this quality should be used in the proper manner it is necessary that moral strength support and protect the mind. The quotation, "The race is not always to the swift, nor the battle to the strong," is merely another way of saying that the race is practically always to the swift and the battle practically always to the strong. Therefore, we must consider strength as one of the qualifications necessary to achieve victory in the battle of life. Life and the battle for success, as well as happiness, is a continual and never ending struggle. The weak can never hope to achieve victory except by the method of making themselves strong.

However, much depends on the point of view of the individual in regard to the battle of life. If the individual considers this battle as one of real war where every man's hand is arrayed against him, and where the aim of his competitors is his destruction or death, then he is continually beset by fear and is subject to despair and humiliating defeat. If on the other hand he can visualize life as a game to be played under the rules of fair play and good sportsmanship, and where even the loser has the thrill and enjoyment of playing the game and can always come back and enjoy another opportunity to win a victory, then he is continually encouraged and comforted by his own viewpoint on life, and regardless of his many defeats and disappointments can gradually develop his strength and ability until his ultimate victory is certain and substantial.

Just as in big league baseball, every man cannot be on the championship team and win outstanding success, but practically all of them can be on teams that win a substantial number of games played and are therefore victorious to that extent. Even the players who are on the bench for an entire season have the opportunity to put themselves in condition so that the following year they can be among the active players and do their part in achieving as many victories as possible during the season. It is discouraging and devitalizing to a man's character and is an outstanding evidence of mental and moral weakness to assume the attitude that his fellow men are bent upon his destruction and humiliation. It may be true that his competitors are fighting for an advantage over him, sometimes an undue advantage, but he does not necessarily need to regard them as enemies on that account.

Competitive sports of all kinds are one of the outstanding activities in America, but among these competitors it is rare to find any actual enemies. They fight hard to achieve victory which means defeating their opponents, but there is no rancor or bitterness involved, and sometimes the loser, if he puts up an excellent fight, receives almost as much recognition and appreciation as the winner. It is the quality of the battle that really counts, and if a player is on his toes and always doing his level best, he not only will be given proper recognition, but will in due time become a victor himself. A quitter is always regarded as a coward, providing of course that his objective is worthwhile, and this is the general opinion held by the average individual, regardless of all the excuses and alibis that are made for the weak by the over-sentimental individuals who seem to believe that rewards should be given to those who need them, rather than to those who are worthy of them. Sometimes it seems that more strength is necessary to combat the misguided efforts of those who are supposedly interested in the welfare of the people, than is needed for any other purpose whatever.

In this connection it should be thoroughly understood that everybody in life has to make good in one way or another, and that the rewards of life should be given to those who make good and not to those who fail to make good. While it is true that in this age of civilization we should allow no one to starve, or freeze to death, it is also true that we are under an equal obligation to see that those who are helped in times of distress should be compelled, if physically able, to do a sufficient amount of work to compensate for the help that is given them. It is even more vitally our obligation to see that those who desire work in order to make good in a larger way, should have this opportunity available, not only for work, but for as much work and as efficient work as they are capable of performing. While it is true that individuals should not be allowed to work regularly sufficiently long hours to damage their health, it is equally true that they should not be compelled to work sufficiently short hours to curtail their income and their advancement.

It takes mental and moral strength to accept these fundamental principles and to act upon them in view of the conditions prevailing at the present time. There are millions of individuals out of work, and the maximum hope and expectation of the most optimistic of our people is to see that most of these individuals secure jobs of some kind, reasonably soon. This is by no means sufficient and should never be accepted as a solution of this problem, and it would be an evidence of national weakness to do so. Work is the only means by which the average man can make a living, but we must not fail to remember that it is also the only means by which a man can increase his standard of living. A small number of individuals are able to increase their standard of living through the means of promotions due to increased knowledge and efficiency, but the average man's only hope for an increased standard of living lies in more opportunity for work and the increased purchasing power of his income. This increased purchasing power must come from a gradual and continuous reduction of the cost of production and distribution of the articles which he buys. This is another essential fact that we must be strong enough to recognize and act upon. In the meantime, the average man's only hope of an increased standard of living is to be allowed to work longer and to thereby have the opportunity of making a larger income.

Union labor has right and justice on their side in their endeavor to establish minimum working hours for occupations at a standard wage, but they are hopelessly in the wrong in endeavoring to limit the number of hours that the man actually works. The standard wage should cover a certain number of hours, and this should be true of all employees in all lines, but the worker should be allowed to work longer hours, not inconsistent with his health, at the same rate of pay, so that he could make a larger income, if he so desires. There should be a standard of efficiency in work, but those who could accomplish more within a given time should be allowed to do so, and should receive extra pay therefor. To endeavor to limit all men to a certain standard of hours of actual work and of efficiency, is to take away from their individuality and ability. If a man can do more or better work than another, he should be paid accordingly, but the standards have to be set in order that this would automatically occur.

We must have the still further mental and moral strength to accept the obligation of seeing that no individuals except those who are mentally and physically incapable are ever allowed to become dependent, either upon the State or upon their relatives. If a man is capable of working he should work regardless of his necessity to do so, and it must be understood that the number of individuals who are actually incapable of performing sufficient work to pay for their upkeep and comfort is practically negligible and not even worthy of consideration. We must have the strength as a nation and as individuals to accept these obligations and to proceed accordingly. There is plenty of work to do and the one thing that is necessary is to use common sense in establishing the means by which this work can be provided and then to allocate it properly.

So far as the individual is concerned, physical strength should be regarded as important, but not absolutely vital. Our conception of strength, however, in this connection, should be ability to resist and overcome physical afflictions and ailments, and to really enjoy life from a physical standpoint. Bulging muscles and a strong back are of very little value if a person's heart, lungs or stomach are not in good condition, and our robust and husky college athletes can be over-trained and over-developed so that they are particularly subject to pneumonia and heart disease. A pale anaemic individual who bends over a desk all day long may possibly report for duty practically every day of a rather long life. The real test of physical strength is whether you are able to keep permanently on the job for which you are responsible and do reasonably efficient work at all times. A man does not need any more physical strength than this, but to stay on the job permanently and regularly except for short vacations and an occasional rest period is a rather large order in itself. Of course certain occupations require more physical strength than other occupations, but the essential problem is for a man to find the work that he really enjoys doing. In short, everything possible should be done individually and collectively to keep ourselves in good physical condition, and to enable us to enjoy certain physical activities which we particularly like to engage in, but this should be done casually and automatically, just as we bathe or shave, and we should not continually be worrying about the condition of our health. Always remember that worry is not only an evidence of weakness, but that it always breeds far more troubles than those troubles over which we worry. Most of the things that we worry about are things that pertain to the future and a large majority of them never actually happen, so that most of our worry is absolutely useless and it also tends to make us unfit to meet the situations that actually do arise.

This does not mean, however, that we should ourselves do nothing about the circumstances and conditions that cause worry. If any troublesome situation arises, either in the present or in prospect for the future, we should first do all that is humanly possible to correct or remedy the situation, or to meet it properly, and then dismiss from our minds the worry and the bother connected therewith. Weak individuals usually worry about the future because they have not the strength of character to *do* anything about it, and they prefer worrying to corrective action. The strong man is usually so busily engaged in trying to correct troublesome conditions or situations, that he has not the slightest time to sit down and worry about the situation itself. It is true that many problems have to be thought out and this may involve physical inactivity, but it presupposes an exceptional mental activity in planning what to do physically. The strong man sincerely asks the question of himself, "What am I to do?" and then proceeds to sincerely answer the question. The weak man uses the same words, but as an evidence of despair, and with no real intention of trying to solve his problems.

Physical and mental activities are closely related, for it must be our brain that tells us what physical acts to perform and what words to say. Speech is a physical activity but the words that we speak or write must come from the brain. For instance, we may think of a very excellent reason why our banker should lend us a certain sum of money for expansion of business. The action may be sound economically and favorable to profits, but we must physically speak the words, sign the papers, and perform our regular duties in the business to accomplish the actual result. In fact, thought, speech and action are so closely related that it is sometimes hard to distinguish between them in point of priority, but it is always important to remember that thought should always come first and that speech and action should follow their orderly processes.

Mental strength consists largely in determining the wise thing to do, but it is often necessary that moral strength be brought into play to first determine the right thing to do, for unless a thing is right it cannot possibly be wise. Physical strength may be used for evil purposes just as well as good ones. Even mental strength has often been perverted for unworthy aims and ambitions, but moral strength is the saviour of civilization and of mankind. These three elements of strength, therefore, should be used always in conjunction with each other. Moral strength should determine what is right, mental strength should determine what is wise, and our physical ability should be used for the accomplishment of these worthwhile purposes.

Weakness has brought more disaster and suffering to the world than any other one failing of humanity, but it has almost always been moral weakness that was the principal cause of our afflictions. Strength has brought most of the good that has come into the world, but unquestionably it has been the element of moral strength that has brought about the really beneficial and desirable progress of the human race.

Be strong, therefore, in all things, but let your physical actions wait first upon a considered decision as to what is right, second as to what is wise, in following out the right course of conduct. In this way we will not only do what we should in the way that it should be done, but we will be strong and self reliant citizens of a strong and glorious country.

September, 1935

COMPARISONS

THERE is an old saying that comparisons are odious, and while this is not necessarily true in all cases, it is relatively true due to the state of mind of the individual making the comparison. In a small number of instances comparisons are made which recognize the progress and development of an individual with due credit being given for their advancement both as to character and capability. This is as it should be. Unfortunately, however, in most cases comparisons are made along lines that are not of advantage to the individuals who are their objects. There is a tendency to compare performance with expectations. Most individuals have the habit of expecting too much of other individuals just as soon as they show any signs of development and progress.

Parents expect their children to secure as good marks at school as they have done previously. If they receive better marks, that is fine, but if they receive lower marks, regardless of the fact that they are qualifying marks, then the parents are disappointed. This in spite of the fact that qualifying marks are at percentages within the capacity of the average child. The parents, however, desire their offspring to be better than the average. This of course is impossible for if all the children were better than the present average, then the marks that they reach would automatically become the average.

The above refers to the acquisition of knowledge, but has very little to do with the development of character. If parents would pay more attention to the development of character traits in their children and endeavor to have them establish a high mark along this line, it would be far better for the children even if they only received passing marks at school.

The tendency in comparisons is illustrated by the general statements, "I am as good as anybody else," and "I wish I were as rich as John Brown,"—John Brown being a mythical figure of someone who is better off financially or otherwise. In other words there is a tendency to accentuate the quality of our moral and mental attainments while at the same time we depreciate the quality and worth of our possessions, our health and our freedom. Almost every man believes that he is as good as most other men, but there are a very limited number that desire to do anything to show that they are better than other men.

When it comes to questions of character most individuals are content to receive a passing mark, even if in some cases this mark itself is not deserved, but when it comes to questions of power, influence, money or possessions practically every individual would like to be listed well above the average. In taking this attitude they are themselves making a comparison that is not only extremely odious, but is distinctly against their own welfare.

Character traits are the most important things in life. Without them it is impossible for a man, regardless of power, place or influence, and especially regardless of wealth, to acquire happiness or even contentment. Everyone in life is actually seeking happiness even if they are too ignorant to understand that this is so. When a man desires wealth, influence, power or possessions it is solely because he thinks these things would make him happy, in ninety-nine per cent of all cases. The mere fact that he gives others reasons for desiring these things is superficial and misleading. People do not deliberately set out to acquire things that will make them unhappy.

In social life particularly comparisons are the breeders of many little disturbances that are totally unnecessary. Mrs. Jones compares herself and her possessions with Mrs. Brown and Mrs. Smith, but in the following manner. Mrs. Brown is wealthy, but not prepossessing, so Mrs. Jones compares her possessions with those of Mrs. Brown. Mrs. Smith is relatively poor but beautiful in face and figure, so Mrs. Jones compares her personal charms with those of Mrs. Smith. There are many other methods of comparisons, but the usual thing is for individuals to compare themselves with those who are more favored and never with those who are less favored.

We take for granted full and complete sets of fingers and toes, of arms and legs, of eyes and ears, in functioning condition. It is only when we lose the use of any of these physical possessions that we appreciate them fully and completely. We do not go around loudly proclaiming the fact that we are not afflicted with heart disease or tuberculosis, but we certainly make the welkin ring with our lamentations if we do acquire such afflictions. The average man or woman should be glad to be alive in such a wonderful world, in full possession of their faculties and with a sound and wholesome body. The enjoyment of life has to do largely with our attitude and viewpoint, and this is created to a very large extent by our methods of comparison. If we would continually endeavor to develop our characters so that we could truly say that we were above the average then we would have something to be really proud of.

Possessions are things that we can take pleasure in according to our capacity, but are not something to be proud of unless we honestly earned them through our own sincere effort and ability and are using them for the good of humanity as well as ourselves. This does not mean that we share our possessions with others, but it does mean that we use them so far as possible to bring benefits to others as well as to ourselves. For example, if a man has a comfortable and well furnished home he should make that home an example of what a home should be and it should be the training ground for the children of the family, with the purpose of making them into sound, honorable and worthwhile men and women. The family, themselves, should be able to enjoy each other and have a good time among themselves.

The moment that a home is turned into a place of continual entertainment of outsiders, or the moment that the members of the family begin to feel that it is necessary to go somewhere else in order to have a good time, then the home is losing its true character and is not being used for the purposes for which it is really intended.

Most families have a certain amount of friction between certain members almost entirely due to their faulty system of comparison. People expect too much of each other merely because they are closely related and they feel that their close relationship gives them certain privileges and rights which actually can never be bestowed on anyone. There are certain privacies and certain rights that belong to individuals merely because they are human beings, regardless of their age, although age has something to do with certain other rights and privileges.

For example a child, regardless of age, is entitled to know why they should do certain things and refrain from doing others. Also each member of a family is entitled to be treated as an individual as well as a part of the family, but also every member of the family should have a part of the family responsibility.

Children when grown have a duty to see that their parents do not suffer privation or hardship, if they can prevent it, but this certainly does not mean that a married son or daughter has any duty whatever that compels them to live in the same residence as the older people. Every married woman and every married man are entitled to a home of their own no matter how poor or insignificant. If intelligence is used, families can be supported as economically and comfortably separated from each other as they can living together. The real trouble is that it seems so much easier to live together than it does to use this intelligence. This has resulted in hurt feelings and sometimes mental suffering on the part of certain members of such families. An older man or woman would almost always rather live in one comfortable room that they could call their own, than to be compelled to live with a son-in-law or daughter-in-law. The few occasions where such arrangements have proved satisfactory only proved the rule. A younger man and woman just married would be far better off to also live in one comfortable room than to go to live with the old folks and everybody would be much happier in almost all such cases.

The young business man or young working man look at those above them in position and think how satisfied they would be with the other fellow's job or income, but as soon as this is acquired they immediately compare themselves with someone still higher in position or income. Very seldom do they compare themselves with those who are not so well off.

Men should be ambitious and should desire to progress, but their ambition should be to acquire more responsibility and to be actually more important because of their developed capabilities, rather than thinking about more money or more power. If we take care of our development, both as to character and capability, the financial and business rewards will almost automatically take care of themselves. This does not mean that a young man, so to speak, should "hide his light under a bushel," but it does mean that he should make himself so valuable that he would just have to be promoted to a better job. This may not always be done with a particular business entity but it stands good for the general field of business. If a man makes himself too valuable to be kept on a mediocre job, then he will inevitably secure another job.

One of the principal methods by which a young man can make himself qualified for promotion, and one that secures the quickest results, is the development of his own character and intelligence. This development rests entirely with the man himself. He may have to wait a considerable time to have the opportunity to develop along actual business and technical lines, but he doesn't need to wait one instant to start developing his intelligence and his character. In the long run this will prove most beneficial along financial and business lines, and, which is far more important, it will make him into a real man, capable of doing many things for the benefit of others, and finally, which is the most vital and important point of all, capable of acquiring happiness and enjoying life to its full measure.

One of the chief elements to consider in striving for success is the amount and the kind of work to be performed. It has to do both with the element of time, and the element of efficiency, but it also has to do with the element of sincerity. No one can be truly said to be vitally interested in succeeding unless they are willing to perform all of the work and the kind of work that is necessary for their success. Individuals who are not dominated by these characteristics have a tendency to excuse themselves by false comparisons. They claim that they have worked hard for many years and see no apparent results, whereas other individuals have progressed further and more rapidly. In making this comparison they either fail to take note of the additional effort, time and determination that were the prime factors in the success of the other individual, or else they deliberately choose someone for comparison who was especially fortunate, or who had the backing of his family or friends and their resources to aid him in his undertaking. They never mention the thousands of individuals that have worked harder than themselves and achieved less.

Success can be had only by paying the price therefor. The rule for success is simple. It is first necessary to decide what you desire to accomplish, and this goal should be placed as high as a person's native intelligence can envision. This does not mean that the further acquisition of knowledge and experience may not impel them to a higher and better goal at a later date. But it does mean that they must have common sense understanding of their aim and destination in so far as they are capable of visualizing the future.

The second item necessary is that the goal must be satisfying when actually reached. This does not mean that ambition will come to an end, but it does mean that they shall not have to admit that they made a mistake in deciding what they wanted.

The third element is that it should be a worth while object in itself and destined to bring benefit to others as well as to the individual concerned.

The fourth item is that there shall be no qualifying restrictions as to time, effort and intelligence that are to be used to accomplish their results.

A man must necessarily be willing to work just as long as it is necessary to arrive at his goal. He should be willing to work just as hard and as much as it is necessary to accomplish his objective in the shortest possible space of time through use of proper and honorable methods, and, more important than all, he should be willing to use every atom of his intelligence to achieve his purpose and be willing to constantly endeavor to enlarge the scope and efficiency of his intellectual processes. If a man does not desire to do these things then he is deluding himself in believing that he desires to achieve success. What real difference does it make if a man does work harder and longer than some other person to achieve the same results.

All successes do not follow in exactly the same manner. Some individuals require a long time to get on a sound basis but develop much more rapidly thereafter, while others develop their success more quickly, but do not press forward thereafter so steadily and persistently. Some individuals' ambitions are gratified when they arrive at a certain point, while others press onward and upward consistently from one goal to another.

The man who is actively occupied with his whole heart in struggling for success along proper and honorable lines has neither the time nor inclination to compare himself with other individuals except from the standpoint of bettering his own character and abilities.

The modern young man has more available help and assistance in bettering his condition than was ever thought of in the old days. Everybody is actually eager to help a really ambitious man on his way. It should not be considered as a contradiction of this theory when business or professional men, through a series of tests, endeavor to find out whether a man is really ambitious, or whether he is merely anxious to arrive at a certain point without the hard work necessary to rightfully earn success.

When we consider what the immortal Lincoln had to undergo in order to achieve his legal ambition, walking miles to borrow books and then sitting up late at night, after a hard day's work, studying all alone by the light of a tallow candle, it gives us a fair impression of what the ambitious young man of that day had to do to achieve even the ambition to acquire knowledge, and it impresses upon us forcefully the wonderful opportunities that are available at the present time to men who have only a small portion of the desire to succeed that animated our ancestors. Men worked hard in those days and they were proud of their ability to do a man's work.

The modern man's work may be different and not so arduous, but a man can still give plenty of value received on a man's job by exerting himself and putting his heart in his work. He should do this not merely because of the benefit to his employer that might result in promotion, but in justice to himself and to his own character and self-respect.

The main idea is to see how much work we can do in this world and not how little, to do our best work instead of a mediocre substitute. Finally, to do this day after day steadily and consistently, in the meantime using all of our endeavors to increase our intelligence and experience to thereby broaden and expand our responsibilities.

The simple rule, therefore, condensed is this; first: fit yourself for responsibility by developing your character and your capabilities. Second: seek responsibility (it will not be hard to find for most men will be found shirking it). Third: be proud and happy because of the responsibilities which you have succeeded in securing and discharge them with all of the intelligence and ability in your possession. Fourth: measure your value to the world by the amount of responsibility placed upon your shoulders which you have handled, and will handle in the future, to the satisfaction of others as well as yourself. Fifth: endeavor to impress upon other worthy individuals the importance of following these same rules and regulations, being firm on principle but considerate and tolerant of other people's mistakes when they are actually trying to do the right thing.

When you have done this you will have arrived not only at the status of a real man of real importance in the world, but you will have also arrived at a point of development which will enable you to remain reasonably happy and contented under the most trying and adverse conditions. You will have no apology to make to your family, your friends, your community, or your country, and the only piece of advice to give to such a man is merely this, don't ever "get the swell head" because you know you are good.

October, 1935

APPRECIATION

APPRECIATION is a quality that is not only a great aid to happiness but is also very beneficial and helpful to all those with whom we come in contact. In other words, it is one of the traits of character which, while classified as a secondary trait, is extremely important to our own happiness as well as the happiness of others.

Appreciation divides itself into many classifications, chief of which are: appreciation of things, appreciation of services, appreciation of love, appreciation of people, appreciation of life, and appreciation of the Creator.

The appreciation of things is closely aligned with appreciation of services, but for practical purposes it means appreciation of things that can be seen, felt, tasted, or smelt. Wonderful scenery, beautiful pictures, flowers and trees, birds, animals, the majesty of the mountains, lakes, rivers, and the great seas and oceans, the sun, the moon and the stars, the green grass, the beauties of the cultivated land. There are literally thousands of nature's gifts to human beings to make life more beautiful, more pleasant, and more interesting.

It is true that nature also has provided dangerous places, dangerous and annoying insects, reptiles, animals, and even dangerous fish and birds. It is true that nature has provided danger from wind, rain, sun, and disease. Danger, however, is one of the necessary adjuncts of human existence, and life is supposed to be a continuous battle. To think of life as being otherwise is suicidal. We have to perpetually battle evil from the moral standpoint, ignorance from the standpoint of wisdom, and it is only natural that the same thing should apply to physical things.

Danger gives a certain amount of zest to life, and even the so-called coward accepts thousands of adventures that are dangerous without realizing his own temerity. Walking along public highways and crossing city streets are dangers of the first magnitude in our own Country. We have made dangers of our own for human kind far beyond what nature had already provided. Mankind has continually struggled to combat wild beasts and to eliminate as far as possible poisonous insects and reptiles. In the early days certain small animals, insects and birds often threatened the destruction of crops which were necessary to feed the people. Danger is ever present in one form or another and if we live it is necessary that we continually fight for our own existence.

If we desire safety, we must fight for it, and we must fight even harder if we desire convenience, comfort and a reasonable amount of happiness. In spite of all the obstacles presented to us by life itself, however, the appreciation of things makes it possible for us to enjoy life to a large extent even if we are poor or in ill health.

The poor man may not have the same opportunities as the rich man to travel and to see many of the beauties of nature. The average man who is compelled to live in a poorly lighted, ill-ventilated, and not-too-clean habitation, usually regards himself as very unlucky, but it is usually true that he lives in a large city, the very wonders of which should provide a never ceasing source of interest and enjoyment. The massive quality and beauty of a great "sky-scraper" is a wonderful thing in itself, which literally millions of individuals journey from far points to merely observe. The poor man has thousands of things of this nature at his very doorstep. It is useless to argue that the poor, especially if they be hungry or cold, are in no position to appreciate the wonderful things of life, for it is this very appreciation that gives them courage and strength to conquer the hunger and the cold and to overcome the obstacles to their personal well-being. It is the same thing as saying that the unfortunate man cannot use the only weapon that he has to help him to attain a better position in life.

A proper appreciation of the wonderful things that both nature and man have provided for the free use and enjoyment of all human beings is the one thing that is needed to make life seem worthwhile to a large number of people. It would prevent most of the suicides, and eliminate a large part of criminal activities.

The most important distinction is that we should appreciate those things that we possess or that we have the use of. Just as soon as we begin to appreciate only those things which are not our own, or which we do not have the privilege of using, we are embarked upon a permanent road of unhappiness. This does not mean that we should not strive to acquire worthwhile things that we may desire, but it certainly does mean that we should not remain unhappy and discontented during the period of striving. If a man is unable to secure a certain amount of enjoyment and happiness with what he already has, no matter how little, he is exceedingly unlikely to attain content or happiness by the acquisition of other things, no matter how large or valuable. Appreciation, therefore, of the things that we have or can use is the key note to happiness.

Appreciation of services covers much more than merely

what is commonly included in that term. Services are usually thought of as pertaining to paid employees or to people who serve food or attend to our personal needs or desires. In its broader application it pertains to all of those individuals who furnish us instruction, amusement, or recreation, to public employees and to the vast army of individuls who render services gratuitiously for reasons of love, friendship, sympathy, kindness, consideration or courtesy. Some of these services can be paid for with money, but most of them can only be repaid by like services to others when such opportunity presents itself.

The appreciation for these services does not need to be hypocritical or over-enthusiastic, but on the other hand it should not be casual or treated as of no consequence. A sincere and natural expression of thanks for services rendered is the most satisfactory appreciation that can be given to those who render services. Even if the service itself is of no value and may actually interfere with your enjoyment or comfort, it should be recognized and appreciated if the intent is sincere and honest.

Many parents have had the experience of having gifts made to them by their small children, such as a bunch of wilted dandelions as a bouquet for mother, or a ten cent pair of cuff links for father, and sometimes appreciation for such trifling gifts has been much larger than if those gifts had actually been valuable.

Even third or fourth rate members of the theatrical profession have at least some good points on their program and we could applaud the fairly good material, at least in a small measure. This applause might not enable them to hold down their jobs or keep the show going, but it would give them a certain amount of encouragement and help in their struggles.

We have given these two extremes as examples but it applies to all other relations of human beings and even animals. Appreciation of services performed is one of the first requisites of a real gentleman or gentlewoman.

Appreciation of love naturally includes affection, friendship, kindness and consideration. The man who loves his fellow men does not classify this love in the same category as the love for his wife, children, or other members of the family, but it is nevertheless one of the most profound and deep expressions of love that has been demonstrated to mankind.

It is not necessary that we have the same degree or the same type of love for humanity that we have for those who are closest and dearest to our hearts, but it is important that the love for those who are essential to our happiness should not interfere with our consideration and kindness to the rest of the world. Love is a beautiful and wonderful thing in itself, but the nearest approach to the love for the Divine Creator is the love that we bear His children, which includes all humankind.

Love is not purely a possession of humans, for many animals evidence this in such form as to almost make ourselves feel ashamed. When we consider the quality of the devotion of a dog to its master it often makes our own feelings seem entirely inadequate to the occasion.

Our appreciation therefore of the love that we are able to feel for others can only be surpassed by the appreciation of the love that others feel for us. A man or woman may feel that they love deeply, but they practically know that their love cannot equal that which their mother has for them, except in a perfectly mated union between a man and a woman, which by natural law takes precedence over other forms of love and is entirely separate and distinct from love of family, friends, and humanity.

Appreciation of love of Country and of God can be used to minimize the obstacles that often seem insurmountable between the love of Country and the love of God and humanity. Men were not made to fight each other but to help each other, but we must remember, as stated heretofore, that life is a continual battle and that the human race is slowly but steadily learning to cooperate rather than antagonize. We must not be too discouraged if final results along this line are not obtained in our own generation. We can merely look at the progress that has been made in the past and realize the eventual outcome.

We must appreciate the feeling of loyalty and patriotism held by citizens of all countries and endeavor to turn this along lines that will benefit not only their own country but all others as well. This has been done along medical and scientific lines for so long that it has been taken for granted. It only remains to develop the same procedure along economic lines as well as that of personal relations. If we truly love God we will be patient and forbearing and merely do all in our power to assist in bringing about pleasant and profitable relations between all the nations of the earth. The more we love our own Country and the more we love the Creator, the more we will assist in bringing about the desired result.

Appreciation of people is probably one of the hardest lessons that we have to learn. Even the worst individuals usually have some good qualities, and can in course of time acquire a still larger measure of them. We can all broadly recognize that different nations have certain qualities which are worth while emulating. We can also recognize some States and some communities have decidedly progressed along definite lines that are for the benefit of the physical, mental or spiritual welfare of their citizens.

The hardest lesson to accept is the fact that almost every individual citizen within our own communities should have a definite appreciation of his place in the scheme of life and of his efforts and accomplishments. Without employees no one could be an employer, and without servants no one could be a master. Each definite individual has his own place to fill, and our appreciation should take the form of seeing that each individual has the opportunity to progress according to his own native ability, his ambition, and his previous record.

Appreciation of life itself is all-important. It practically consists of an appreciation of the items which we have previously mentioned but is exemplified fully by the joy that comes from just being alive and able to partake of the sufferings as well as the joys and pleasures of existence, of being able to participate in activities that fail as well as those that succeed. In other words, to be a living and active part of the general scheme of life.

Appreciation of the Creator and of the magnitude and magnificence of His creations is entirely distinct from the love of God, itself. It has to do with a recognition of the supreme power, wisdom and accomplishment evident to our own senses. It is one of the first requisites to an appreciation of all of the other items that have been mentioned and without it mankind would be little more than a human clod upon the surface of the earth. It is the all-important evidence of mentality and physical attainment as well as that of a spiritual nature. Almost all human beings have this appreciation to a larger or smaller degree, but it should be used to guide their actions and to fortify their spirits for the battle of life, so that in very truth God will be on their side in the battle, and it will be His will that finally shall be accomplished.

November, 1935

DECISION

THE quality of decision is defined in the dictionary as follows: The act of reaching a fixed opinion; the quality of being fixed and firm; determination.

The power of making a decision is one of the most essential aids to success and to happiness. We are all familiar with people who never know what they really want, who usually refuse to take the responsibility of making definite decisions, and in the few cases where they do make such decisions are never satisfied with the results proceeding therefrom.

While it is true that a large number of people make decisions arbitrarily without full knowledge of facts, and often with prejudice, there is a certain definite satisfaction and helpfulness that comes to other individuals in knowing just where the others stand. If a man knows that another man is a definite enemy, he is far better able to make his own plans accordingly than if he is building upon the foundation of a fluctuating and unstable friendship.

A man may be totally wrong in his opinion, but the fact that he sticks to it and really has an opinion of his own, derived from his own brain, is a stabilizing influence upon the actions of his fellow men. Things that are definite, regardless of how bad they might be, are always easier to combat and to overcome than things that are uncertain and extremely changeable.

It is an enormous undertaking to build one of our modern skyscrapers, or one of the great dams that have been erected in various portions of the Country. Great obstacles have to be surmounted, but because the engineers are dealing with certain stable elements, it is possible to plan with certainty upon the job being completed and even to approximately estimate the time required for completion.

Suppose, however, that a large portion of the concrete or of the structural materials were known to be unstable and uncertain, that these materials had the power to change their nature and refuse to do the thing expected of them. No engineer would use such material, for permanent structures must stand the tests of time and strain.

Human beings with weak and vacillating minds are composed of just such material as we have mentioned. They cannot be counted on by either friend or foe. They are almost certain to be of a different mind one day than they were the previous day, and they are practically sure of having an entirely different opinion, if possible, by tomorrow.

Ignorance and prejudice and the opinions originating from them are two of the greatest obstacles to human progress and happiness, but they are far easier to conquer, subdue and eliminate, than the elusive quality of indecision. It is better to have wrong opinions than to have no opinions at all.

A physician may battle a disease or an affliction, regardless of its deadly quality, just so long as he can correctly diagnose the case, but if his diagnosis reveals one cause one day and a directly opposite the following day, he is unable to make any progress whatever toward the elimination of the disease, and the cure of his patient.

A man with wrong opinions may be a dangerous adversary,

but at least he is one man, and you only have to look in one direction to see him. The man with the changeable mind, however, is just as hard to overcome as three or four adversaries who continually hop around, fighting from the back as well as the front, and, seemingly acting the part of a friend, help to give you the knockout blow. It is impossible for individuals to lay their plans correctly upon the foundation of other individuals who may be their friends one day and their foes the following.

We have given considerable space to the comparative qualities of those who have decidedly wrong opinions and those who have no opinions at all. In other words, between those who are capable of making a decision, however wrong, and those who are incapable of such definite action. We have done this particularly because there is a great trend at the present time in the direction of people being so broad-minded that they might just as well have no mind at all.

Even the question of morals has become surrounded with so much confusion that many comparatively intelligent and high-minded people are advocating or sponsoring movements or activities that would heretofore have been regarded as criminal or illegal. The most damaging part of this so-called broad-mindedness is that the activities undertaken are understood to be for the welfare of the people.

Following the present trend to its natural conclusion would mean that at certain periods the entire wealth of the nation would be equally distributed among all the people and that all power would be lodged in the hands of politicians, deceptively labeled government.

This means that the incentive to progress and acquire personal possessions would practically be eliminated and that the standard of living would not only drop to a low point, but would remain there, as there would be no incentive for those who had the ability to raise the standard of living to make the effort.

In older days the forcible taking away of another person's property was called by its right name, theft, but in this modern era the forcible taking away of property through the means of taxation and solely for the benefit of certain classes or individuals, is called liberal and is done in the name of the welfare of the Country. Taxation was founded for sustaining the legitimate expenses of government, but it was never intended to be used for the purpose of taking away from one to give to another.

The average honorable man at one time made his decision in regard to theft and dishonesty. It is particularly important that that decision remain unchanged regardless of all the sophistry and camouflage surrounding the question at the present time.

Every man of average intelligence knows that he is not entitled to benefits which he does not actually earn through his own efforts. That is a very simple statement and it is just as simple to carry it out, unless the element of selfishness enters in.

It is also necessary to remember that the people are supposed to support the government and that it has never been the duty or responsibility of government to support the people. Government is not able to support any portion of the people for the simple reason that government has no funds of its own and has to be actually supported itself.

Government is an employee of the country's citizens. Yet this employee assumes the right of taking money that is not needed for purposes of government and using it for the support of individuals, whereas this particular problem belongs to the individual citizens of any community. It is not our purpose to go into this particular subject further in this article. We are merely using this example to show the necessity of making a decision and then sticking to that decision when we know it is right.

Another example has to do with the cancellation of airmail contracts by the government without hearings to determine fraud. A still broader example was the arbitrary reduction of the value of the dollar. We must remember that expediency and need do not justify dishonorable or illegal acts.

We must also remember that the *power* to do things that are unjust in no way lessens our responsibility when we commit such acts. A strong and powerful man has the power to kill or maim a weaker individual, but certainly this does not justify such action. So a national government has power to do many things that are both illegal and dishonorable, merely because the people have no recourse.

Governments necessarily have to be given arbitrary power, under certain circumstances and conditions, for the preservation and safety of the nation, but the endeavor to prolong and expand such exceptional powers should be the very reason for ending them. In other words, those who are willing to continue with emergency powers for any great length of time and those who are determined not to release such powers are the very individuals who are dangerous when they have such powers at their command.

There are many individuals who have decided that this Country should be autocratically ruled by a central government at Washington. They have made their decision and they are sticking to it, regardless of the fact that they are wrong in principle and unfair in attitude. At least, however, they have the power of decision.

It is important that individuals who believe in real liberty should stick just as uncompromisingly to their own decision, which they have previously made, to the effect that they desire the citizens of the nation to be its real rulers.

Just as soon as questions of political persuasion, of personal gain, of religious intolerance and of prejudices create a situation where those who believe in liberty are divided and set against each other, it creates conditions where the believers in autocratic government can throw their support to one side or the other for their own selfish interests.

Just as soon as the liberty which most Americans believe in thoroughly, has been taken away from them, we will find that religious and political liberty will also be lost shortly thereafter.

Freedom of religion and autocratic government are directly and permanently antagonistic and will forever remain so. It is necessary that individual citizens make their decision upon the great fundamentals of our system of free government as embodied in the Constitution of the United States. If they do not desire liberty they have a perfect right to renounce it, but they have no right whatever to refuse to recognize that it is the intention of many individuals in powerful positions to take this liberty away from them. Everyone has a perfect right to give up privileges and rights of their own, but they have no moral right to evade their responsibility and their duty to their country and its citizens.

Every individual has innumerable personal decisions to make during the course of his lifetime. It is exeedingly important that all decisions be made as promptly as possible and not put off or delayed beyond the time necessary for him to arrive at a knowledge of the facts and circumstances necessary to making the decision.

If such facts and circumstances are not available and if it is necessary to make the decision without such facts, then the decision should be made from the standpoint of common sense, upon the basis of the facts that are available. It is important to understand that decision should always wait on the facts, when such facts are obtainable, as that is the only just method, but it is our duty as individuals to proceed to obtain the facts as promptly as possible.

There is no such thing as a neutral or waiting attitude as between right and wrong, justice and injustice, honor or dishonor, for waiting often allows the wrong to triumph and justice to be dethroned. It even allows honor to become dulled and sometimes eliminated. It is always wise to do the thing that is right regardless of the consequences.

Expediency is often used as a method of self preservation, or of selfish attainment, but where expediency becomes necessary for this purpose, and the path of honor, of justice and of self-respect is not followed, then the thing that is preserved is not worth preserving, and the individuals benefited do not deserve such benefits, but in fact deserve punishment.

The average individual has to decide upon so many things that it is impossible to catalogue the different items. There are things that pertain to his relation to his home and relatives, his wife and family, his friends and acquaintances, his job and his business associates, his social activities, his political and religious activities, his personal responsibilities and his responsibilities to others. Even such matters as cleanliness, health, safety, comfort, pleasure, etc., are all matters of continuous and personal decision.

The man who knows what he wants out of life, and who has the character to strive for only those things which are worth while, has an inestimable advantage over other individuals, both in the power of decision and the time required to make such decision. In effect it gives him a much longer life to live than the man who does not know what he wants, as his life is fuller and more complete, more active, and more interesting.

The chief and most beneficial result, however, is that it enables him to secure so much more happiness out of life. Happiness is the real result that everyone is striving to attain and the man who knows what he wants can find that happiness more quickly and in much larger measure.

Besides, if he makes decisions promptly, using honor and common sense as an aid, then, even if the decisions are wrong, he is able to more quickly correct his mistakes and to get back on the right path.

It is again worth while, however, to warn individuals that quickness of decision is not a virtue when it is not based upon available facts. In such circumstances quick decisions may be unjust and dishonorable, as well as very unwise. As a matter of fact, if an individual is not willing to ascertain facts before making his decision, then his decision does not really amount to anything and could not really be called a decision at all, for he has simply refused to use his brain rather than having used it for the purpose of making a decision. In other words, a decision must be the result of an active use of our mentality and not a refusal to use such mentality.

This may sound very complicated to the average individual because he thinks of all the decisions that he will have to make in the future years. One simple rule can be followed, however, that will make the process itself simple and effective. We only need to use our common sense and to decide upon each question from the standpoint of right or wrong, eliminating any personal consideration, prejudice or benefit entirely from the picture.

If we would only decide upon our actions with the same intelligence that we would use in advising some other individual in similar circumstances, where we were not personally concerned, we would then find that the path would be smooth before us, and that our efforts to conduct our affairs with intelligence and with honor were successful, progressive and productive of self-respect and happiness.

December, 1935

IMPORTANCE

IMPORTANCE is defined as the quality of being important, which is explained as of much significance; momentous; bearing weight or consequence; of high standing; pompous.

We thus see that the word itself possesses a quality that gives standing to the people, principles and things referred to as belonging in this category. Technically, therefore, when we say that a man is of little importance it still establishes his standing as very high merely because he is at all important. This should never be forgotten in connection with our use of the word when referring to friends and acquaintances, to principles and ideals, to the activities of life and to other things of interest. We can readily understand that this divides itself into two classifications, those things which are important to one's self and those which are important to others or to the world.

It is not so usually recognized that there is another division of its meaning into two classifications. First, those things which mature judgment and time prove to be important, and second, those things which only seem to be important due to egotism or selfishness. We can easily recognize that a person's character, their high standards of conduct, their code of ethics, their loved ones, their friends, their community, state and nation, are all extremely important to the individual, and the fact that we place this importance upon such things is of great importance to the entire world and to the progress of mankind, while, on the contrary, the placing of importance upon such things as pomposity, egotism, unearned place, position, or power is not good but harmful, both to the individual and the world at large. It is important for us to realize that we should not consider our own importance except from its relation to the responsibilities devolving upon us which are being successfully discharged and to the affection, friendship, and esteem which we have worthily earned from others. In this connection, it is desirable to point out that only a relatively few individuals have an exaggerated idea of their own importance and that this article will concern itself mainly with the large number of individuals who have been led to believe that they were practically of no importance whatever in the general scheme of life.

To those of us who really desire to make this world a better place to live in, it should be extremely important that we concede a certain small measure of importance to every human being regardless of how poor and lowly his station in life might be, and how little public or private recognition he might have received in the past. The hard-working honest laborer who delivers a good day's work, the poorly paid school teacher who conscientiously tries to educate our children, the vast army of industrious citizens that live and die without getting their name in the papers, without securing public recognition of any nature, and in many cases without having even their own loved ones feel that they have accomplished much in life, merely because they have not proved to be what is called successful, are the foundation and the backbone of our nation. Wealth, power, glory, recognition and reward are actually given to a very limited number of individuals and so far as wealth, power, glory and reward are concerned, this is naturally and mathematically as it should be, for such things are comparative and are really noticeable to a large extent because only a very few achieve them.

Recognition, however, is something that can be given with satisfactory results to everybody concerned. In fact it might almost be said that recognition of good work well done, or the absence of such recognition, measures the difference between a certain amount of happiness and an equal amount of despair. The great trouble is that all of us are too sparing or miserly with our recognition of the importance of other individuals and their work. Especially is this true in the very place where such things should be most fully recognized and appreciated.

The average housewife cannot seem to get any great thrill out of being told that her husband has learned to accomplish a larger result in his capacity for work, but begins to be interested only if there is an indication of increased pay or promotion. The fact that the husband has both the capacity and the desire to increase or better his output should be one of the most cheerful and encouraging items of news that could come to her ears. If she would only think this through to a conclusion she would realize that her encouragement and her appreciation would impel the husband to consistently better his performance, and that this would inevitably lead to beneficial results along the lines of income as well as security, position, and standing.

There is a standing and a class in workmanship that is applicable to even the most minor position, and the housewife should be a support and a help to her husband in bettering his qualifications, knowing that this would eventually also better his position and his income. From her own point of view, therefore, she should take a great interest in her husband's work and in his performance of that work. On the other hand we will assume that a housewife is an especially good cook, a really efficient housekeeper, or a capable, competent mother. We do not mention all of these qualities as pertaining to the same individual, for that would be almost too good to be true, and if a man should be so fortunate as to have discovered and appropriated a girl who combined all of these qualities, or who eventually attained them, then he should consider himself extremely lucky. It is important to realize that the successful handling of any one of the above attributes is something that requires not only intelligence and application, but also a reasonable amount of imagination and ingenuity as well as a lot of very hard and sometimes extremely distasteful work.

The average man will, shortly after marriage, be extremely complimentary about the product that the good cook has brought forth, and overlook her mistakes and shortcomings, but five years later will sit down to a wonderfully prepared meal and simply consume it without any favorable comment whatsoever, as if it were his inherent natural right. He not only fails to realize that he is being favored by Providence, but he is even critical if any of the prepared articles do not measure up to the highest point of perfection previously reached by his better, and in this case much better, half.

This same thing holds equally true with keeping the house in a comparative degree of order, especially when there are children to be considered, and it also holds true in a greater degree to the rearing and training of children. Most of this training has been left to the exclusive care of the mothers of the nation and their successful efforts along this line cannot be praised too highly or recognized too much. The mere fact that children are brought up to school age with such a relatively few needing to be classified as brats or general nuisances should be an outstanding tribute to the mothers of our nation.

There are dozens of other little items that have to do with

home life and family that should never escape recognition and appreciation and this is especially true in regard to the children in the family.

A grown man or woman may be helped considerably, but children actually thrive on recognition and appreciation, especially when connected up with a reasonable amount of responsibility, according to their maturity and ability. Always remember that responsibility automatically gives a feeling of importance to a child that the most outstanding demonstrations of love and affection sometimes fail to achieve. Responsibility also means an undiluted and higher form of attention, and children crave attention so very much that even the best of them will at times do naughty or provocative things merely to gain the attention of those they love. We do not mean to infer that this applies exclusively to children, for many of us grown-ups pattern after them in this regard.

In the world of business the humblest employee should be made to understand that he is a relatively important cog in the machinery of business. This can often be done more readily by showing him what to avoid and how it is possible for him to waste money, to cause damage or delays, or to cause the loss of money, rather than to attempt to show him how he, as a minor individual, can actually make money for his employer. A modern business is more or less like a piece of machinery and it is very important that every portion and particle of this machinery function efficiently and regularly. The number of individuals who fail to respond to having responsibility placed upon them is so small as to be relatively negligible. Here again we find that the placing of responsibility automatically increases the feeling of importance of an individual in the general scheme of the business world.

It is unfortunate that the stressing of importance of an individual job and his manner of handling that job is usually reserved for those occasions when an important promotion takes place. It would naturally be silly to go into such detail of the technicalities of any job to such an extent that the individual taking over the job would feel afraid to undertake the duties involved therein.

The wise and efficient method is to actually take an interest in the individual, stress the importance of the work, but make the individual understand that he is the more important of the two because the work is his responsibility. It should be possible to say with perfect truth that you have confidence in his ability to handle the job. This would not only create a spirit of co-operative and efficient effort but would serve to give him a certain amount of confidence in himself that he might otherwise lack.

The net result of making any employee feel his own importance is in almost all cases an increased effort and a far, far better result, which in turn leads to profits for his employer, and should lead, naturally and inevitably, to better work and a larger income for himself.

The world is slowly coming to a realization that comparatively few men desire to be placed under the classification of servant, and that even the humblest employee would do far better work and secure far better results if he were made to feel a part and parcel of the institution itself and a co-worker with the very highest ranking individual in the company or business. Profit-sharing alone will not bring about this particular feeling completely. There must, in addition, be a recognition of the individual and of his place in the scheme of things, and this can only be given as from one individual to another.

Many employers often wonder why good workmen so often do not aspire to bettering their work, and the answer can be found by the discovery that good work, when it becomes habitual, is not praised or recognized but just naturally expected.

We should understand enough about human nature to realize that if we criticize bad work whenever it comes to our attention that we should also praise good work when it comes to our attention no matter how often or how regularly this might occur. We thus give an incentive to the good workman to do better work, an incentive that is often far more strongly appealing to the individual than the opportunity to make a little more money.

Almost every thinking individual realizes that these things are facts about human nature and yet so few individuals take advantage of these facts. Possibly one of the greatest obstacles has been a false or pretended interest in the quality of workmanship and not a sincere interest in the man himself or of his progress. Another of the facts of human nature is the ability to distinguish between sincerity and hypocrisy, and in many instances uncultured and sometimes uneducated workmen have derided the efforts of their superiors to put something over on them, as they would term it, whereas a real interest in the men, in their progress, and a real show-down on the results that could be achieved by their full and complete co-operation, would have brought about an entirely different state of affairs and have resulted in benefits for everybody concerned.

When we turn to the social phases of life we find innumerable complications surrounding importance. It is not desirable or necessary to dwell upon the large group of individuals who continually strive to make others feel that these particular individuals are important. This procedure eventually defeats its own ends, and the average man and woman are usually fed up with some individual or individuals in their own particular group that are continually striving to stress their own individual importance. Here especially there is a reason for trying to approach something like sincerity in our personal relationships. Instead of hypocritical catering to individuals that we do not admire or like, and in some cases even despise, there should be a sincere and straightforward endeavor to gather together people who have somewhat similar tastes, character, ideals and ambitions. In other words, if people could refrain from inviting, or accepting invitations from, individuals in whom they have not the slightest interest and for whom they have no real friendship or affection, the world would suddenly turn out to be a better place to live in.

Sincerity should be the keynote of social intercourse, but unfortunately it has become almost as far removed from sincerity and frankness as the realm of politics. The social problem is too diversified to even attempt to discuss, even if we used the entire article for this purpose, but unquestionably each individual should decide for himself or herself that unless they can act sincerely and naturally with a given group, regardless of its size, that they do not belong in that group, and it would be for their own happiness and peace of mind if they refrained from entering into its activities.

When we approach the field of politics and of public office we find a system built up which allows in advance for propaganda, mud slinging, vilification, slander, and even falsehood, and which then drops the subject and pretends that no one is expected to take such things at their face value, and, in the case of candidates for office, the opposing candidate usually tenders a message of congratulation. In this particular field the individual concerned is not supposed to tell how wonderful he, himself, is, but he is at perfect liberty to hire or persuade other individuals to do this for him, with the understanding that they will be rewarded later if the candidate is successful. This subject also is of too large a scope to crowd into a single article, but also, in this particular case, the most important element is sincerity and the ability to rely and depend upon an individual's word.

Practically speaking, a man's importance should depend upon his past record of achievement in things worth while, his present performance and his future probabilities along the same lines. The man who desires to advertise himself by words should be relegated to the scrap heap, but the man who is willing to let his record speak for him should be given further responsibility.

Each individual should place most importance upon a high and strong character and the next thing in importance should be the building up of this character and this strength. Holding fast to this determination will build for anyone, whether he be rich or poor, a record that is worthwhile and of which he can be proud, and that record will, in the final analysis, speak for him with far greater force and with a greater degree of efficiency than any words that he or his friends might utter.

January, 1936

TRUTH

TRUTH is almost universally regarded as exceedingly complex, but in its general application it usually proves in the final analysis to be very simple. Truth is always dignified and worth while regardless of its subject matter. The dictionary definition of truth is as follows: agreement with reality; eternal principle of right, or law of order; veracity; fidelity; fact.

In order to simplify the understanding of truth it is desirable that we consider it as an accurate statement of knowledge that has been proved to be correct. Opinions may be true but opinions, themselves, can never be regarded as truth without the proper proof. Expert knowledge may be true or partly true, but cannot be accepted as truth until proof has been made of this knowledge. In other words truth is not a statement of facts that can later be proved, but it must essentially be a statement of facts that have already been proved. If we would recognize this essential relation of proof to truth, we should avoid many pitfalls in our search for knowledge and incidentally in our search for happiness. There is an old saying that "The truth cannot be learned in a day." As a matter of actual fact the truth and the whole truth is something that mankind will probably never be able to compass. We can only add to our knowledge of truth day by day and year by year.

It is the extent to which we desire to acquire this knowledge, and the methods pursued to obtain same, that counts in the life of the individual and of the group. The best examples that can be given of the unbiased and eager search for truth are the scientists who devote their lives to the search for scientific facts. They accept truth as such, regardless of their preconceived opinions and they deny the label of truth to those things which have not been proved. Some of them have even gone so far as to deny the existence of a Supreme Being, for the simple reason that they are unable to prove with their formulas the actual existence of the Creator.

They fail to take into their calculations certain facts which have been proved over countless years. One of them is the distinct and undeniable desire and need of all peoples at all times for a God to worship, and the absolutely necessary explanation of the motive power of the universe. If there is one thing that seems to be absolutely demonstrated it is that brains and the breath of life are necessary to recreate themselves in human beings. We have seen how mankind, with the use of a very small portion of the brain with which the Creator endowed the human race, has harnessed the forces of nature and made them obedient to the will of men. It is only common sense that is needed to perceive that there is an immeasurably higher mentality, and a Supreme will behind the creation of the universe and its continued existence and order.

When we leave the field of science, however, and turn to other activities of the human race we find that truth is searched for in the large majority of cases for a purely selfish purpose. The business man may be searching for a new product or invention with the ultimate aim of larger profits. The scholar may be searching for evidence to bolster up his preconceived opinions.

The politician may only be seeking for such truth as may enable him to attract votes, and the social reformer may be seeking for a method of making the people happy, comfortable, and prosperous without the aid of common everyday work or labor.

The Bible recites the fact that a man was told "In the sweat of thy brow shalt thou eat bread." As the years and the centuries roll by the experience and the progress of mankind seem to point inescapably to one point, to such a remarkable extent that it should now be accepted as a fact. Happiness is the supreme goal of the human race and of each individual member thereof. It was happiness from which mankind was banished by the Creator when Adam and Eve were driven out of the garden of Eden. The fact that the human race was not at that time destroyed seems to indicate with absolute conviction that mankind should thereafter have the opportunity to earn the right to happiness as individuals. The majority of people seem to regard this allocation of labor as a punishment that was sent on the human race. If we could only recognize the fact that it was not a punishment, but a pathway to happiness, the world would be a far better place to live in.

The human race was not intended to stand still and do nothing. It was intended that at all times they should build for the future; build protection and defenses for safety, build homes for convenience and comfort, build up the race, itself, through the mating instinct, build up the mentality of the individuals, and finally and most importantly build up the character of the human race, so that they would deserve happiness. In order to build this character of the race it has been necessary for individuals to build up their personal characters, and it is the building of such characters that has been the purpose of all the rewards that practically all religions have offered to their followers. There is an aspiration of the human race for happiness that could have only been implanted by the Creator, Himself. It is universal and the only difference between human beings in this respect has to do with the difference in the methods they use in striving to attain happiness.

The criminal will rob and murder in order to secure things which he desires, while the noble individual will sacrifice many things to attain higher objectives, but all are interested in the same goal. This goal is to be reached through one avenue and one only. It has been reasonably proved that idleness is not only a bad thing for the individual but that his idleness is also a bad thing for other people. The world has been reasonably content and satisfied when the world has been at work building, and it has always been dissatisfied when a large portion of its population, either rich or poor, have been idle. It may be true that in certain individual instances there have been certain tribes or peoples who have seemed to be content and satisfied without a great deal of work. This particularly pertains to certain savage tribes in regions where nature has been lavish in furnishing food for the population, without a great deal of effort on the part of the individuals. It is safe to say, however, that civilized human beings, having tasted of the joys and benefits of greater knowledge, would never be content with the same things that satisfy the savage.

It is true that the acquisition of knowledge or of truth brings with it a certain amount of suffering as well as benefits, but men have proved that they have always been capable of suffering for the attainment of worth while objectives. Certain parts of the human race may retrograde and descend to a lower depth of civilization, but it has been impossible for them to be satisfied with their lower status. When we mention satisfaction, contentment and happiness we mean things that a man aspires to and will work for. If he is not willing to work for such objectives then it cannot truthfully be said that he aspires to them or even desires them. The true criterion of a man's desires is the amount of work that he is willing to put forth to attain that desire. Work does not only mean labor from the standpoint of physical exertion, but it especially means the use of the brain and the heart. The brain gives direction to our physical work and the heart gives sincerity and emotional impulses. Some emotional impulses are incorrect and improper and should be subdued, but most of the work of the world has been done by men and women in all ages for the support of their loved ones, as well as themselves. This is a true and impelling motive, but it has as its background the endeavor to arrive at the goal of happiness.

Idleness usually creates discontent both in the idle person and those who see him idling. It is not intended that the impression be conveyed that an individual should work longer and harder than nature gave him the capacity for. It is intended to convey emphatically the idea that a certain reasonable amount of physical and mental labor should be concluded by every normal human being within each year. The hours do not have to be the same each day and the energy expended may vary from time to time. Regular hours, regular meals and regular recreation and resting times have been used as a convenience and benefit rather than imposed upon us by outside forces.

In the final analysis, however, work has been given to us as the *road to happiness;* physical work to keep our bodies in proper and normal condition and to help in building for the future; mental work to facilitate and expand our progress and our productivity; moral work, or heart impulses, is needed to round out the picture, to make us aspire to higher, better and nobler things, and to lift humanity to an ever higher plane of existence.

Physical work is more or less circumscribed by the inevitable realization of facts or the discovery of truth. We are practically only at the beginning of an understanding and a knowledge of our physical universe, but people are usually willing to accept proved physical facts without cavil or antagonism. In this field, therefore, there is only a question of the diligence with which we pursue knowledge and not its final acceptance when ascertained.

Mental truth is far more complex not because of the facts themselves, but entirely because of the mental reactions of millions of individuals. In other words a man can refuse to believe those things that he does not desire to believe, regardless of proof, or he can believe things that are not proved. This has entirely to do with the individual's personal attitude toward truth and can never alter the facts themselves. Many intelligent men and women have decidedly different viewpoints about certain conclusions and certain evidence, regardless of the fact that these entirely opposing viewpoints or opinions are based upon the same set of facts. This is caused almost entirely by their super-imposing upon the original foundation of truth, another foundation composed of individual prejudices, emotions or selfish desires. This automatically results in building the structure of their lives upon a false foundation and, which is equally important, this false foundation obscures or completely hides the real foundation of truth. It is not possible to discourse upon the thousands and millions of individual reactions, processes of thought, or ultimate conclusions in the minds of that particular number of individuals. It is sufficient to say that it is vitally necessary that we be truly sincere in our search for the real truth, and that we endeavor to keep our personal desires and interests from obscuring what would otherwise be plainly evident. Moral work, while gaining ground steadily over the centuries, sometimes in particular periods seems hopelessly muddled and confused. We are at this time passing through such a period.

In the early stages of civilization the welfare of the people was given scant consideration by those in high authority. Today we have a world-wide desire on the part of civilized governments to convey the impression that those in authority are deeply concerned with the welfare of the people. It is a strange and peculiar thing that all of the schemes and experiments put forward by reformers, regardless of whether they be called dictators or politicians, are put forward ostensibly in the interest of the common man, the average individual, and yet the result is in every case to take something away from the common people rather than to add to their benefits.

In Russia and in America the consumer, which represents everyone, is made to pay the price of all experiments. The individuals who benefit are only the small group that happen to be in power or authority, or fortunately placed to profit. In every case there has been a lowering of the living standard of the population and not a better living standard.

The World War and its aftermath of uncertainty, speculation and increased desire to get something for nothing, undoubtedly have had a great deal to do with the lowered conditions of the average citizen of the civilized nations, but in its broader sense this condition has been brought about due to our departure from the road to happiness. In the case of the World War a large part of the most energetic and active members of the population departed from work and started fighting. After the war was over there was a long period before these men who survived were placed in the avenues of work. There was a certain period thereafter when general progress was made, and the world seemed to be recovering gradually from the effects of the war. This was not true in all countries, but it was true in a general sense. In America particularly there seemed to be a rapid recovery of prosperity and it looked as if we were in for a long period of increasing prosperity. Profits were quite large in business and stock speculation increased rapidly with prices rapidly mounting higher. Taxes were sufficient to run the government and in addition to reduce Federal indebtedness. The fever of speculation increased rapidly and many farsighted individuals realized that stock prices were too high and that a crash was inevitable. When this event occurred in October Nineteen Twenty-nine, the effects were felt immediately in every avenue of business.

Business began to retrench and unemployment became a rapidly mounting problem. Naturally, when hundreds of thousands of workers ceased to be producers, their purchasing power declined and the effect of this on business was further retrenchment and more idle employees. The vicious circle continued until there were considerably more than ten million individuals who had lost their jobs. These events are not remarked upon from the standpoint of a financial history but merely in order to show the importance of regular and steady work to the average man and woman. The fighting millions in the war were off the road to happiness because they were not working at a productive job. The idle millions can be considered as not a result of the depression, but the cause of it.

Those who are interested in the welfare of the citizens of their own country should lend their efforts to furnishing work to every able-bodied individual. The heart goes out to those individuals who are suffering, but it must be borne in mind that it is the method employed to end this suffering that decides whether an individual is really interested in the welfare of his fellow men, or whether he is merely saying so for the effect that it might cause. Work is what the people need and to offer them anything else as a substitute is to prolong their misery and humiliation and add to the burdens of the rest of the citizens who are employed.

Regardless of all subterfuges and explanations, it is an inescapable fact that those who are employed must support, directly or indirectly, those who are not employed, if they are to live at all. The government and the wealthy classes have no income sufficient to possibly support the idle millions. In fact, the Government, itself, has to be supported by the people. If we are searching for moral truth we must inevitably conclude that the chief duty that we have as regards our fellow citizens is to see that they are given the opportunity to work and thus remain independent. Emergencies may require that a man stay in bed, either at home or in a hospital, when he is really ill, but to endeavor to insist that he remain idle for an undetermined length of time merely because he has been idle through an enforced situation would be considered not only cruel, but idiotic.

It had been demonstrated in Nineteen thirty-one and Nineteen thirty-two that the chief obstacle to a return to normal conditions was the idle millions whose purchasing power had dwindled to practically nothing. The natural thing to do would have been for Government and business to get together and provide them with jobs so that they could support themselves. Practically every man realizes that Government and business have been drawing apart rather than getting together. It is the business world that is supposed to furnish jobs for the idle and it would seem the natural thing for Government to ask business how it can help in making these jobs possible. Everyone realizes that these things have not been done, but most people do not realize that Government and business must work in cooperation and mutually helpful agreement to create work for so many idle men and women. It is a sufficiently hard task even with this cooperation, but is practically impossible without it. There are many individuals who never have worked and never intend to work but we do not believe that it would be the truth to say that they never will work. We are of the firm conviction that no able-bodied man should be allowed to live upon his fellow men and that he should be compelled to at least work sufficiently to pay for his own living.

The measure of the sincerity of our regard for the welfare of our fellow men, and especially our fellow citizens, is the measure of our efforts to provide them with real work and a real job, not some other time, but right now, and thus keep alive the real spirit of America within the hearts of our citizens. Independence has been our heritage, it has been the source of our personal pride and self-respect, and without it other things have been valueless. Let us be sincere therefore, and not only sincere, but active in our personal and individual effort, no matter how small, to furnish these fellow citizens of ours with the work that will make them independent and give them back their pride and self respect. Work that will enable them once again to hold up their heads and to participate in the progress and prosperity that must inevitably come to us when work is resumed all over the Nation. Let each of these individuals have the heritage that is rightfully his, the right to work, to have a real job, and to hold up his head and be proud of being a free American citizen.

February, 1936

PERSEVERANCE

THE quality of perseverance is one of the most wonderful qualities of mankind and it is also a quality that steadies and stabilizes the individual. Perseverance is usually regarded as a long, slow, steady progress towards a definite goal and it is practically never associated with spectacular or rapid financial attainments. It is probable that the general impression created is derived not only from the hard work associated with perseverance, but with the courage and self-control that must be inevitably associated with it.

It requires a great amount of courage to persevere in the face of great obstacles and to overcome them, but it requires still greater courage to persevere in the face of defeat and disaster and to continue the struggle for eventual success. Self-control comes into the picture to the largest extent after success has been achieved and it is probably the most important element entering into this particular quality. Self-control impels a man to carry on to greater heights and to refrain from lessening his own self-discipline, the discipline imposed upon him by dire necessity prior to his success. Self-control is also necessary to keep him from becoming egotistic and conceited. Perseverance has to do with work but, as in most qualities of human beings, can be directed in wrong directions as well as right ones.

Perseverance in a worthy cause merits the highest praise, but perseverance in an unworthy cause likewise deserves the greatest blame. Perseverance always means a moving forward of the individual regardless of the surface indications and therefore the individual who perseveres in following the right road inevitably climbs upward and his character is continually being built up along the right lines. Perseverance in the wrong direction just as inevitably means a steady and relentless movement downward with a consequent lowering of the individual's standards, character, self-respect and morals.

Perseverance is usually associated with work but we have often seen this quality used for the purpose of avoiding work, obligations and responsibilities. We have occasionally noticed individuals who actually put forth more energy to avoid work than the actual work, itself, would call for. It is evident therefore that many individuals are prevented from exhibiting the quality of perseverance for other reasons than an actual aversion to work itself. The reason for the failure of such individuals is almost entirely due to the desire to evade responsibility. They have qualities and capabilities that would enable them to climb higher but they prefer the safe and easy road of being content with small success, and letting others pass them and take up the responsibilities which they themselves should have assumed. The fear of responsibility is much broader and deeper than the desire to avoid work. It will therefore be seen clearly why courage is an essential part of perseverance.

Perseverance truly can be said to be the road to the highest point that an individual can attain in life. It does not permit the individual to stop merely because he has accomplished a certain task. It spurs him onward so that, long after his own particular needs are satisfied, he shall continue so that he may provide to many others the means of satisfying their own needs and desires. It will thus be seen that perseverance is not only beneficial to the individual but that it is also of even greater benefit to mankind.

Every individual who arrives at a point where his own needs are satisfied must of necessity from that point on give more largely to others, in the way of opportunity and a chance for their own perseverance, than he could possibly give to himself. The rich man who continues to build up his own fortune must of necessity give more than he receives. The only really worth while things economically are opportunity and independence. The rich man has attained these but he must continue to give them to many others in order to increase his own wealth. It is not possible for him to do otherwise regardless of his personal desires in the matter. After a man has attained independence there is really nothing worth while for him to do except to help others to attain their own independence and these others must necessarily be those in whom the quality of perseverance is deeply imbedded.

Both nature and civilization put human beings to the test in order to discover whether they are real, whether they are strong, whether they are courageous. Perseverance is an answer to this test. What does it greatly matter whether a man takes ten years or thirty years to arrive at a state of economic independence? What does it greatly matter about how many obstacles he must have overcome, how many failures were recorded, how many disasters overtook him, just so long as he arrives at his goal with his honor, integrity and self-respect unsoiled? It really does not matter except that the man who has overcome the most obstacles and faced the greatest problems must of necessity be a stronger, bigger and better man than those who have had an easier time.

Self-control is also an important element. Self-control does not mean without emotion, but it does mean that a man must be calm and steadfast. Self-control does not mean lack of adventure, but it does mean reliability, common sense, calmness and courage in the face of danger or disaster. The early pioneers of this country were undoubtedly full of the spirit of adventure, romance and emotion, but they were also noted for their calmness, steadiness, courage, dependability and self-control. Their leaders were chosen because of the possession of a larger quantity of these very qualities. They did not necessarily choose the best rifle shot or the best horseman for a leader, for all of them were more or less proficient in such matters. They chose the steady man, the reliable man, the man who would not only persevere himself, but encourage and demand that they also persevere, in order that they might reach the end of their journey, safely if possible, without too much discomfort and danger if possible, but nevertheless to reach it.

Perseverance has been exemplified down through the ages and in all walks of life. Jacob worked fourteen years for Rachel's father in order to win Rachel for his bride. Many modern young men continue to ask some young girl to marry them and will not take no for an answer, with the result that in many cases the girl finally decides that if the young man really cares that much about her that it would be the part of wisdom for her to change the no into a yes. Probably one of the most outstanding examples, however, are the very young individuals commonly called infants who can persevere practically interminably until they get the proper attention. When human beings grow to manhood and womanhood they are supposed to cast aside childish things, but if they would only imitate a small baby in its relentless pursuit of a purpose, they would probably never have much to complain about as to what they got out of life. The only essential difference is that a baby, owing to its helplessness, has to cry for what it wants while a grown individual has to work for what he or she may want. The same persistence, the same determination, and the same perseverance would achieve success for practically any human being. Above all we must remember that a baby knows what it wants and is not going to be satisfied until it gets just that. It refuses to accept substitutes unless by some chance the substitute happens to be more satisfactory than the original objective. On the other hand grown people have a habit of accepting very poor substitutes for opportunity and independence, and that is the particular reason why so many individuals fail to accomplish their objectives.

Life, itself, is an endless and eternal battle and one of the greatest dangers confronting the human race is ignorance. We have all the facilities available to properly educate our children but our educational system fails to include the most important thing in life. A code of ethics, teaching honor, loyalty, courage, justice, fair play, consideration for others, etc., would do far more toward making real men and real women out of our children than all of the other teachings combined. Perseverance is the answer to this particular problem. Our schools must be made to progress and not to stand still. We must continue to persevere until we shall establish a school system that will turn out men and women with a high code of ethics. Some of our schools and colleges, instead of teaching children the difference between good and bad and showing them why they should follow good, seem to prefer to say, "Now this is good and the other is bad, and you are at liberty to take your choice." This they call academic freedom. They fail to teach the children that no one has a right to think wrong things any more than they have a right to do wrong things. It is not necessary to know or to experience evil in order to appreciate good and yet many of our educators feel that it is necessary to state both sides of the case just as they would both sides of a political controversy. In effect it is much the same as saying that it is perfectly proper to argue as to whether the right arm and hand or the left arm and hand are more valuable, and because there are arguments on both sides to insist that it is also perfectly proper to argue whether it is better to have two arms or one, to have one diseased arm and one good one or two good arms. We have merely mentioned these things in passing as an illustration of the fact that we must continually persevere not only in our homes, but in the schools and colleges and that we must continually raise their standards and not allow those who are paid for this service to actually cause them to be lowered.

Communism, for example, is not a theory of government at all and no one should be allowed to discuss it in our public or private institutions of learning except as a horrible example of what should not be done. There is absolutely nothing to communism except a desire on the part of those who have nothing, to forcibly take away the property as well as the influence of those who have something. It is a well-known fact that those who are in control of property, business or government actually own that property, business or government. So far as Russia is concerned, instead of property being owned by several million individuals, as under the Czar, all the property in Russia is now owned in all essential respects by a small handful of men who are at the head of a so-called government. As a matter of fact, the people themselves are virtually owned by this same small group of men. If they want to take a man's property and use it for their own purposes they can do so. If they want to take a man's life to further their own interests, they can also do that. And all this without any hope of retaliation on the part of those injured, or recompense for the injury. To say that this is a theory of government is so absurd that it is idiotic. To say that it is a rule of the people would be laughable if it were not tragic. The people can rule only by a free expression of their will and if this expression is not perfectly free then it is impossible to say that the people rule. As a matter of fact it is openly admitted in countries where dictators reign supreme that the general public has neither the intelligence nor the ability to rule properly.

In the United States there has been much talk lately of equality, sharing the wealth, but there has been little said on the part of politicians about sharing power. This power, it is stated, must be in the hands of a relatively small group of men, as they are the only ones, according to themselves, who have the intelligence and ability to use it wisely. In this connection we must remember that wealth has only the power to make life inconvenient and to make the common man suffer, but that power has the outstanding and remarkable ability to chop off a man's head and take away his property entirely.

It would not necessarily be disastrous for our government to be possessed of immense wealth in its own right, but we would certainly be heading for disaster if we ever grant government the power to control the actions of the individual, to control his personal and private affairs as distinguished from his property. It would naturally be an economic disaster for government to control business and property, but it would be a much graver disaster for it to control the personal life and the personal actions of men, except to prevent them from committing crimes and illegal acts, as they have previously been recognized. It is useless to say that perseverance shall be diligently adhered to until a certain change takes place in the personnel of the individuals who administer government. What we need to do is to persevere until the people's will shall again, as it was at the time of the founding of this Republic, be made the law of the land and no departures be allowed from this law.

There has been much talk of the necessity of the Supreme Court of the United States being allowed to interpret the Constitution, so as to bring it into conformity with modern conditions. It is our earnest belief that at least seventy per cent of the citizens of America are just as sincere, just as earnest as their forefathers were, in their determination that no central government, no state government or any lesser entity of government shall be allowed under any circumstances or conditions to take away from the individual citizens their personal and individual right to rule their own country and to tell their government what the people want done. They don't want a government and never will want a government that will tell the people what the government wants done.

The Government of the United States as well as the government of the states and cities are the servants of the free and independent citizens of this glorious Country of ours and it is high time that all of us as citizens restate this principle emphatically and without quibbling. If there are to be any changes in the Constitution of the United States they should be in the direction of removing the so-called uncertain phrases and substituting therefor the simple statement that no Supreme Court and no Congress or Executive department is to be presumed to have any power whatever, whether by interpretation or otherwise, that is not expressly stated in the Constitution. If there is any further power that the people, for their own benefit, desire to give to government they can do so through an amendment for that purpose. It is safe to say, however, that when the people really desire an amendment, there is always a tremendous popular clamor for the change, which is recognizable by all politicians or officers of government long before an amendment is submitted to Congress, and practically every member of Congress knows whether an amendment is one that the people want, at the time that he is voting on the amendment.

In order to again reestablish government of the people it is necessary to again proclaim our loyalty as individuals to the same principles that guided our forefathers in establishing the republic. The Constitution of the United States starts off with the words, "We the people" and all that is necessary for us to do is to see that we, the people, pass on all changes that are made in the original document and that if there is a question of uncertainty that this question shall be submitted to the people for their action thereon and not interpreted by any body or any group.

This is in no sense a criticism of the Supreme Court, it is not even a criticism of the Administration or of Congress. It is merely a common sense application of the system of always referring to the people, themselves, in order to establish the fundamental law of the land. In other words, if a matter is so controversial that a large proportion of constitutional attorneys feel that a certain part of a law is not constitutional and another equally large group believes that it is constitutional why not refer the matter to the people, who really make the Constitution. We are not of course referring to questions of constitutional law where the Supreme Court is able to determine just what the law does mean. We are referring only to the very small number of cases where it feels that the meaning is not clear and it then gives its interpretation of what the court thinks was meant by certain phrases.

The plain truth of the matter is that common sense needs to be continually exercised until laws are written in such manner that it is clearly evident what their purport actually is. The people elect their lawmakers and their courts, except in the few cases where judges are appointed, such as the Supreme Court. It is obviously silly to presume that the people want the law-making bodies to pass laws which attorneys, themselves, do not understand. The only question is, are the laws made for the guidance of the people, or are they made expressly complicated so that the people cannot understand them and must refer to their attorneys for instructions as to the meaning? The average man should be able to go to a lawyer of good standing and find out what the law actually is. He should not have to pay a lawyer merely for the purpose of finding out what that particular lawyer thinks the law means.

No law should be allowed on the statute books that cannot be comprehended by the average intelligent man, and this will never come to pass if we allow lawyers to write our laws for us. To achieve this result requires the utmost perseverance. It is not a matter of days, weeks or months. It must necessarily be years, and perhaps many years, before the people eliminate all laws that are not clearly indicative of their meaning and substitute therefor laws written in intelligent English, as used by intelligent men and women. A great part of the laws on our statute books might as well be written in Greek or Latin so far as the average man's understanding of them is concerned.

The first and initial step must be to elect business men to our legislative bodies, men who will write the laws in business and social language, instead of what is called legal terminology. Competent lawyers could then be consulted as to technical points of law, but they should not be allowed to make any changes that would confuse the meaning. Practically speaking, the phraseology of our laws would be far better if they were written by professors of English at our Universities than if they were written by the best legal minds. The people should be able to ascertain from any competent attorney the real meaning of any law and no attorney should ever be compelled to give an opinion. Language was invented for the purpose of making things clear and not for the purpose of confusion.

It will be clearly seen why perseverance will be so necessary to solve this problem, for the average man in our legislative bodies who is not a lawyer seems to think that it is necessary to turn the actual writing of laws over to those who are versed in the law, itself. This is exactly contrary to what should be done, for most of the so-called legal terminology is confusing instead of clear to the average man.

For the average man perseverance must be a continuous, robust and active, as well as common sense, application of his energies to accomplish things that are worth while. Many immigrants from other countries have come to America with no equipment except hope and indomitable perseverance. They have been handicapped by lack of education, by poverty-stricken conditions, and by lack of native intelligence, yet plain ordinary perseverance has not only enabled them to acquire wealth and standing but also to acquire education and real intelligence.

Perseverance means a continual going forward in spite of obstacles. When failure comes it means starting over again with renewed determination and without loss of hope. When success arrives it means not being content to stop at that point but to continually strive to offer opportunities to others who have not as yet succeeded, but who have the desire to do so through their own efforts. By doing this a man achieves his own success in fuller measure, and, which is far more important, he helps many other individuals along the road to success and thereby multiplies the benefit that he brings to his community, his state and his nation.

March, 1936

ARTICLE TWENTY-FOUR

ADAPTATION

ADAPTATION is a very vital human trait sometimes being
necessary to preserve life. It has never been given the importance that it deserves largely because the quality has been
to a great extent universal. There are two distinct meanings
to the word; one signifying adapting one's self to conditions and
circumstances and the other adapting circumstances and conditions to one's needs or desires. In its general application it is
more often used to signify the necessity of an individual adapting himself to changed circumstances or conditions.

Strong men are usually able to adapt themselves to changed
physical or financial conditions while at the same time refusing
to let their minds or morals be swayed by their surroundings.
A man may do menial work and for a time find it necessary to
take his place in the class of the very poor and unfortunate,
but if he is strong he only regards this as a temporary measure
and does not do things to cause him to lose his own self-respect.
As a natural result he emerges from his privations and sufferings stronger than ever before, while at the same time he can
understand and appreciate the failure of weaker individuals under similar conditions.

There are a great many people who feel that because it is

necessary to adapt themselves in some measure to the ways and methods of other nations, groups or individuals with whom they have contact or association, that it is also necessary to adapt their mentality and their morals accordingly. This can only be classified as the advice of weak-minded individuals to those whom they consider as weak as themselves.

As a matter of actual fact the white race has been a strong race for a long period of time and wherever the white race has penetrated it has succeded in carrying with it, its own code of mentality and morals. While this code of conduct and of morals has been by no means perfect, it has established a respect and appreciation for the white race that is universal. As a matter of actual fact, probably the worst thing that can be said of the white man, with the exception of one who is a real criminal, is that he has "gone native" and succumbed to a looser standard of morals and of conduct.

The white race has taken its traditions, its own history, its own standards into practically every corner of the world, and has endeavored to live up to these standards, while at the same time it has not endeavored to enforce them upon other people except in those respects where it was necessary in dealing and trading. It is true that there have been many acts of aggression and exploitation on the part of many white men, but at all times there has been a more universal acceptance of moral as well as mental responsibility than on the part of other races. It is also true that this moral and mental responsibility to a code of conduct has been built up gradually over thousands of years and that many white people were at one time in a state of semi-barbarism.

These things are mentioned only to bring out the essential fact that strong peoples and strong individuals do not need to bow to the force of circumstances and conditions, except temporarily, and that determination and persistence, re-enforced by a code of conduct and morals that is consistently raised higher, can be counted upon, as demonstrated by past history, to overcome all obstacles in the way of human progress.

In spite of the confusion existing within the world today in the ranks of the white nations, we must never forget that the status of men is so immeasurably superior, even at the present time, to what it was hundreds of years ago that there is absolutely no comparison. It is almost everywhere conceded that the average man has certain rights. Even in Soviet Russia the things that they have done have been done in the name of the welfare of the people. In spite of the present situation, therefore, the outlook is by no means hopeless, for we will undoubtedly advance much further and faster during the next three hundred years than we have during the past three hundred. This advancement will be due, however, to the strong individuals who are able to adhere to an increasingly higher standard of conduct and morals.

The demagogue and the charlatan continually prate of the welfare of the people along economic lines, while at the same time they endeavor to evade the moral responsibility, not only of the leaders, but of individual citizens. There is much talk of the welfare of the people, redistribution of wealth, enemies of society, exploiters of the public, paternal government, but there is precious little talk of honor, of fulfillment of obligations, of personal responsibility and of experimentation with the experimenter's own money instead of that of the general public.

There is a veritable mania at the present time for telling other people how they should spend their money. Even government wants to tell business men and private individuals just what they should do with their own property and pass laws compelling them to take their suggestions and advice. This probably invades one of the most precious avenues of liberty when looked upon from the viewpoint of the average man. The farmer and the laborer may actively resent, but will not combat, influences that tend to limit their income or that cause them losses in one form or another, but if anyone undertook to tell them exactly how they were to spend any part of the income which they did receive they would be told where to go in no uncertain terms. Yet, as a matter of fact, excessive taxation is merely a means of government forcing business men and private individuals to spend their money in a certain manner with no hope of any return whatsoever. Under such circumstances it is not a case of business men adapting themselves to changed conditions and circumstances, but it is a case of not knowing what the circumstances and conditions actually are to which they are asked to adapt themselves, and sometimes it is a case of adapting themselves to conditions which will speedily end their existence as business entities. Adaptation has to be made to something that is real and tangible and which promises continued existence. Otherwise it could not be called adaptation at all.

The individual should adapt himself to changed conditions and circumstances, to physical environment, to weather and the elements, but he should never suffer his standards of mental and moral conduct to be affected thereby. It is just as wrong to lie, to steal, to repudiate obligations and to forsake our duties and responsibilities in one country, as in another, in cold as in hot weather, and with one person as well as with another. In adapting ourselves, however, there is one particular point that is exceedingly important and that is bearing our adaptation without complaint or grumbling. This does not mean that we should not criticize government when criticism is necessary or advisable, for government is the servant of the people and not its master, but it does mean that if we have a duty to perform, a hardship to undergo, that we should go through with it and get it over without making those around us miserable because of our complaints or grumblings or our air of martyrdom. Sometimes the manner in which we do things is far more important than the things that we do. The person who says "How can I bear the suffering that I have to undergo" is very seldom important enough to bother about. The people who are really important are those who seldom complain and who never complain at such times and under such circumstances as to adversely affect the happiness and the welfare of those they profess to love. It took only one small straw to break the camel's back and we as individuals should always be careful to see that we do not add this one straw to the burden of any other individual.

The average individual keeps up a good face before strangers and casual acquaintances, but pours out the burden of his woes to his loved ones and occasionally his friends, thereby adding to the ordinary problems of the people he professes to love the additional burden of his distress and state of mind. Let us resolve that we as individuals will be strong and dependable, that we will cheerfully accept the burdens which others may throw upon us through faultfinding and complaints up to the point where common sense dictates other action, but let us never for one moment consider the bestowing through such methods of even a small portion of our own burden to the shoulders of those whom we profess to regard as loved ones and friends.

April, 1936

CAUTION

CAUTION should never be confused with fear. It has often been thus confused in the minds of many people in many individual instances. Fear is the instigator of inaction or of action born of desperation, while caution is the prelude to intelligent action, regardless of the fact that caution may impel an individual to delay action until a more appropriate time or condition. In other words caution is a common sense reasoning about matters that are to be undertaken, while fear stultifies the reasoning power and makes all action unintelligent if not impossible.

There is a distinction to be made, however, between fear and appreciation of danger. A man may realize that his life or those of his loved ones are in danger and he may be filled with misgivings as to the outcome of whatever action he may take, but this is not truly fear. It is merely an appreciation of danger. Appreciation of danger usually results automatically in action that is more or less intelligent, but fear, itself, usually paralyzes action or makes it ineffective. A man of courage uses that courage to take intelligent action but not to overcome fear, for if fear dwells within his heart courage is automatically excluded.

We have often heard of the courage that is born of desperation, which merely means that the individual has fully realized his danger and for the moment has banished fear and is willing to take the consequences of courageous action. Desperation, however, is the exact opposite of caution. The cautious man will weigh in advance the consequences of his speech as well as his actions. Caution will not deter him from doing the right thing, but it may persuade him to wait for a more suitable occasion.

Caution and fear cannot dwell at the same time in the heart and mind of an individual, for caution is the forerunner of intelligent action and fear is the forerunner of unintelligent action or of no action whatever. It might be said that caution is inspired by a determination to go ahead while fear is inspired by the dread of consequences and the lack of determination to go ahead. In the business world, especially, courage inspires men to accept responsibility, but caution is used, first, to determine the extent of a person's responsibilities and, second, the best and safest methods to be used in fulfilling such responsibilities. When we say the best methods it should be understood that this means the most honorable, the fairest and the most effective.

Most men have a fair amount of what is called physical courage in the face of danger. There are a large proportion of these men, however, deficient in some degree in mental and moral courage, both of which are essential when it comes to accepting responsibility. It is especially along these lines that the element of caution should enter in. Some men will accept major responsibilities with little intent to carry through. It is more or less in the nature of an experiment and if the going is rough they will seek to evade or to escape from their responsibilities. We desire to again point out that the element of caution is present when any individual has a determination to see a thing through and to fully live up to his responsibilities.

Caution does not imply that an individual should demand, or even desire, a full set of rules and regulations covering every conceivable condition and circumstance that might arise. It does require, however, that a man should recognize and understand the result which is to be attained and that he should also understand the vital principles and general course of conduct to be used in attaining the desired results. With such understanding the man's own common sense, his honor and his sense of justice should provide him with the solution of the problems which he must face from day to day.

In considering the angle of justice a man's common sense should tell him that he should divorce the personal element from every situation which should be decided entirely upon the bases of principle and justice. Justice calls for rewards to the most worthy and not to those who are most loved. It calls for equal treatment, in questions of judgment, of our enemies as well as our friends. Not only is caution needed in the initial stages of accepting responsibilities so that they may be thoroughly understood, but it must be constantly present in the fulfillment of those responsibilities in order that we may avoid injustice and harm.

The pretense of caution should not be used for the purpose of an alibi. If honor, justice and right demand action, then action should be taken, regardless of the consequences. This does not mean, however, unintelligent action, and caution is necessary in order that intelligent action may be taken at the proper time so that the necessary results will be secured. It will clearly be seen from the above that caution is a companion of courage, of determination, of fully accepted responsibility and of intelligent action. Caution, therefore, does not belong in the class with fear, timidity, uncertainty, or lack of acceptance of responsibility.

Many people have often thought of caution in connection with lack of courage, timidity and evasion of responsibility, but this is contrary to the actual truth. There is a time and place, for example, to break bad news.

There is a time and place for amusement and for entertainment. There is a time and place for serious considerations, for proper handling of business, for training, for education, and for many activities of the world that we live in. Caution should be exercised, not to eliminate any of the wholesome or pleasant activities of our lives, but to bring them into proper alignment with the duties, responsibilities and sometimes unpleasant necessities that are included in our responsibilities.

We cannot entirely banish mistakes and errors; we cannot eliminate sorrow, pain, suffering and distasteful duties altogether; but we can make life so much more wholesome, pleasant and enjoyable that by comparison it would be practically perfect, and we can make ourselves so strong that neither our distasteful duties nor our sufferings and afflictions would be able to crush our spirit or destroy our happiness.

In order to avoid the larger portion of our mistakes and errors, after we have acquired the determination to go forward and upward and have accepted our responsibilities in the full sense of the word, it is exceedingly helpful to have caution ever present at our side. Impulsive and unthinking speech and action are mistakes in themselves and almost always lead to some unpleasant consequence. The cautious man therefore should be careful of what he says and of the way he says it, as well as careful of his actions and the manner of them.

There is no place in a wholesome and pleasant association and activity of the people for the grouch, the ill tempered, or the intolerant. Neither should there be a place for the individual who refuses to accept any responsibility whatever, but goes on his merry way, hurting other people's feelings, obstructing their sincere efforts, and living upon their earnings. A beautiful young girl may do no work worthy of the name, but her mere presence in the world may bring beauty and joy to enough people to justify her existence, provided that she is not innately harmful, obstructive or hurtful to other individuals. An old man may be incapable of doing any physical work, but if out of his wisdom he can guide and help other individuals along the right road he more than justifies his own existence. Anyone who helps build up the world and the character of individuals composing it, is a helpful influence and is entitled to be called a worker. How much more good we may do, then, if we ourselves are not only intelligent workers, but also help to build up the character and spirit of the people with whom we come in contact.

Many of us have known individuals who were hard workers but who never seemed to lose the opportunity of saying something kind and helpful to individuals who crossed their path, who were ready with praise where praise could be given and have kept silent when there was nothing good to say about an individual, who could see the good characteristics in their friends and loved ones and who did not harp on their faults and shortcomings. Such an individual is not only a really pleasant associate, but he brings cheer and comfort into the lives of many just by being around them. There is no reason why each one of us as an individual should not develop into that kind of person, each according to his own temperament and personality. What counts is not the mere detail of how such things are accomplished, but the real intent upon the part of the individual who wishes to accomplish them.

If we do desire to develop ourselves along these lines caution must be an ever-present companion. It is the necessary preliminary to saying the right things in the right way and doing the right things in the right manner. Caution should be considered as a very effective and necessary instrument in being helpful to others, in accomplishing our objectives that are worth while, and in making the world a better place to live in.

May, 1936

COMPANIONSHIP

COMPANIONSHIP is one of the greatest needs of the human race. Regardless of the variations in type, practically all individuals, civilized or uncivilized, desire companionship to a greater or lesser extent. Practically no human being is satisfied without some other human companionship. In fact, the need for companionship is so great that our worst enemies would be acceptable if no other company was available. This, of course, would not be true if it applied to a very limited period of time as a man would rather be alone for a short time than to fraternize with an enemy. But if two who were enemies were cast away upon a desert island, in most cases they would welcome any companionship whatever and previous enmities could easily be forgotten, at least for the period of their involuntary association. Loneliness is a bitter pill for any human being to swallow and the lack of companionship of some nature practically excludes the hope of happiness from an individual's life.

Inasmuch as practically every individual is either consciously or unconsciously striving to attain happiness, it can readily be seen that companionship is absolutely necessary in order to obtain this objective. Companionship not only brings in its train an enormous number of personal benefits, such as where groups of people are gathered together in cities, towns and villages, but it is sought after and needed even where such benefits are not manifest. Vagabonds gather together for mutual association and the lone wolves of the criminal world seek companionship when they are not plying their trade.

It must be evident, therefore, that if we can avail ourselves of good companionship that we will have made a long step upon the road to happiness. It must be also evident that if we ourselves are not good companions that we are fulfilling very little of our obligation to humanity. There is an old saying that "evil communications corrupt good manners." It should be also just as clearly understood that honorable associations help to improve the character as well as the manners of all of the individuals concerned.

In selecting companionship we should not only select the best that is available to us but we should be particularly careful to see that we ourselves measure up to the quality of our own selection. We should also be willing to forego companionship for necessary intervals rather than to associate with those that are not fit companions for ourselves or those that we love. One of our major duties, however, is to be continually on the search for the proper and helpful companionship, especially the kind that brings out the best that is in us and helps to minimize our unworthy and selfish motives and activities. It is our duty to do this for ourselves and others that we love, but especially is this true in the case of our children or of younger members of the family.

A child is always imperatively in need of companionship and especially that of children or young people of their own approximate age. A child may practically worship an older brother or sister, their mother and father may be regular pals to the child, but this in no way detracts from the necessity of the child having playmates of approximately his or her own age. To deny this to children is to distort and magnify their views about life, for children, especially small children, are so essentially capable of seeing through the character of their associates and comparing everybody else with those that they particularly like or respect. If they have parents who on occasion are children with them they will naturally expect other older people to act in the same manner and resent it if they fail to do so. They will also expect other children to have the same poise and sincerity as their parents, the same good judgment and the same sense of fair play. This would also apply to older brothers and sisters and to other older members of the family. If they have companionship of their own age, however, they will see these other children making the same mistakes and committing the same transgressions as themselves, even if they do not receive the same punishment. When they select certain children as those whom they like and respect this selection would almost inevitably be made upon the basis of merit, and this is as it should be.

It must be realized, however, that children and also young men and women need a lot of companionship. It is not a question of this being advisable but of it being absolutely necessary. It is so necessary, that children will not deny themselves this companionship and if they fail to find good companions they will cheerfully adopt those that are bad and sometimes those that are vicious. It is the imperative duty of parents to see that their children have sufficient good associates, and this sufficiency is not to be regulated by the parents, but by the child. This bears the same relation to the parents' good judgment as that of feeding children. Some children can eat more food than either one of their parents without any apparent ill effects, while other children eat very small amounts, especially at certain age periods. The need for companionship is much more evident in some children than others, but the extent of this need is always evidenced by the child's sincere attitude. It is a mistake for parents to believe that children do not know what they actually need along some lines, especially that of companionship. A child who does not have sufficient companionship for his or her needs is like a child that is being deprived of sufficient food. This is an urge that cannot be satisfied by any substitute. Children are usually fairly well satisfied with the amount of food they get, the clothing that they wear, and the shelter that is furnished them, regardless of their parents' financial condition. They eat everything in sight but they do take what their parents are able to afford. Probably the only rebellion or envy in their little hearts is about candy, cake or ice cream. But one thing they will have and will fight for and that is companionship. They will even go to the extent of deceiving their parents in order to have this companionship and it should be absolutely recognized that if their parents do not see that they have sufficient good companionship that they will inevitably, as soon as the opportunity affords, turn to bad companions. A child may be kept at home and not allowed to mingle with other children in the neighborhood but as soon as he is allowed to go to school he will certainly find companionship and as he gets older will drift further and further away from good companionship, connected with home associations, simply because he has not learned to connect home with companionship.

It is also important to realize that many parents, especially mothers, are sometimes literally starved for good companionship of people of their own age. Individually there seems little that they can do to provide this companionship but if such people would consistently seek for others of kindred spirit, intelligence and character they could without great difficulty be drawn together. The fact that they would be faced with the same limitations as to time, financial condition, and facilities for pleasant associations would be an extra incentive to the necessary arrangements for proper and sufficient companionship.

In the business world there is the same crying need for good companionship. It is a hopeless attitude for anyone to take, to conclude that business associations cannot be made pleasant and companionable. It is not necessary to use the time of the firm or corporation in order to indulge in conversation or activities that detract from your own usefulness to your employers, but a pleasant greeting, a few words of cheer and comfort, a little bit of praise where it is deserved, and a smile for those in whom you are especially interested, does not detract from the efficiency of a working unit but actually helps it to become more efficient.

It is important, however, that a smile, a greeting, or a word of praise, be sincere. In fact, sincerity is one of the necessary qualities for good companionship. It is not necessary for the type of person who is quiet and sedate to bubble over with joy or enthusiasm, neither is it necessary for those who are joyous and enthusiastic to restrain themselves by exhibiting no emotion whatever. Practically all individuals have their own particular way of showing sincerity, and with due allowances this is the way that they should use.

Hypocrisy, on the other hand, is a destructive force arrayed against good companionship. We should no more pretend to enjoy the society of individuals whom we detest than we should pretend to dislike those who are our real friends. However, if unwelcome companionship, from the standpoint of personal preference, is forced upon us, as it so often may be in social or business life, then we should endeavor to use this time to our advantage regardless of the unpleasant association. Almost every individual has a personal knowledge, gained from experience or study, about some one or two subjects and these people are almost always willing to talk upon such subjects, with the consequent betterment of the knowledge of the individual to whom their conversation is addressed. If these subjects are not known they can almost always be ascertained by a few intelligent questions and the conversation directed in the proper channels. There is one danger, however, connected with this intelligent way of making use of what would be called misfortune, and that is that the other person might conceive a passable friendship for anyone to whom they could talk so freely and intelligently about themselves and their own pet hobbies or achievements. We would not recommend this course of procedure to two young men who happen to be violently in love with the same young lady, for naturally their thoughts might concentrate upon her to the exclusion of other and safer topics of conversation.

It can be understood, therefore, that if we proceed from ordinarily good companionship to companionship that is carefully selected and tested that we are well on the way to happiness. For some strange reason such companionship alone tends greatly to encourage and help us in our daily vocations and in our ambitions and would eventually lead us to moderate success and independence. Such associations arouse ambitions for worth while things that have been lying dormant, they furnish an extra supply of courage where courage is needed, they continually strengthen us morally as well as mentally and they provide pleasant and wholesome recreation, amusement and entertainment as well as companionship. Above all they serve to weed out and eliminate bad companionship that would drag us down to a lower level.

Companionship therefore entails responsibility. We have to become more responsible for our own speech and actions and the acceptance of such responsibility automatically builds up our own character and self-respect, without making us egotistical. The same responsibility makes us more tolerant of other reasonably worth while individuals, as to their minor shortcomings and faults, at the same time interposing a barrier between our own selected companionship and the companionship of those who are vile, vicious, cruel or degraded.

It must be recognized that happiness cannot be attained unless we accept responsibility. If we are therefore willing to accept responsibility we can automatically use this to enable us to become worth while companions. Companionship is necessary. It is inevitable. The only real question is our choice of companionship. Our real responsibility lies first in selecting worth while companions, and second, but more important, to keep up our own standards so that any group of worth while individuals would be glad to have us as companions and to freely offer us their own companionship.

June, 1936

VALUES

THE judgment of values is a vital element that affects the security, comfort and happiness of each individual. It is distinctly an individual process although it is often affected by mass psychology and by advice given by others. In its simpler state it represents a judgment of the individual as to what would be best for him, not only temporarily but permanently.

Regardless of the amount of thought and consideration given to the desirability of any course of action, or the acquiring of any material thing, there must necessarily be a desire for a definite result or a definite possession in order to lend value to the result or the object to the individual. There is an old saying that "The Value of an object is in the eyes of the beholder." It might also be said that the value of a future result is in the viewpoint of the individual.

There are many different sets of values upon which we are necessarily impelled to exercise judgment. There is a negative judgment that is oftentimes far more influential than positive judgment. It is the attitude of lack of interest, not caring, not feeling that action or judgment is worth while. This particular attitude is expressed very prominently by the large number of individuals who fail to take advantage of their political franchise. Our forefathers fought and died in order to establish a government of the people, which, expressed tersely, means the right to vote. In spite of this fact a very large proportion of those eligible to vote fail to do so, feeling that it is not worth the effort. These same individuals would be those who would complain most vociferously if the privilege were taken away and many of them would probably be glad to give up their lives to restore it. Therefore, it can readily be seen that the things which we feel are securely possessed are regarded more in the form of a permanent value to be accepted casually, but are accepted as of slight immediate and temporary value because we have become so accustomed to them.

This attitude is essentially that of the man who is sound of body and limb and yet cannot rejoice over this fact and appreciate its value until he is confronted with loss of health or deprived of the use of one of his limbs. Sometimes there is a fleeting recognition of our good fortune in this respect when we see others who are hopelessly crippled or critically ill. In general, however, the very things which are actually of the greatest value are passed over lightly or not considered at all. The healthy functioning of the five senses, lack of disablement, good health, and a sound mind are accepted as a matter of course, but the still greater liberty that we enjoy of being able to decide for ourselves upon questions that affect our own welfare and our honor, are often regarded lightly because we have become so used to these privileges.

Another set of values pertains to knowledge that we have the opportunity to acquire. There are so many branches of activity in this particular field that it is impossible to speak of each one separately. In the business and social world we gain experience and knowledge by first hand observation and personal activities. In the schools and colleges and in the general field of literature and of the news, we learn of other individuals and groups and their activities, accomplishments and experience, covering both the past and the present. In the field of science there are constantly being developed new activities of approach to the acquisition of still further knowledge and experience. The same may be said for the field of government and politics.

Social welfare is gradually coming to the front as a separate field in itself. In this connection we are not speaking merely of services to the poor and the unfortunate, but we are referring to the whole aspect of human relations. In this particular field it may be said that we are groping rather blindly, a rather large portion of the people endeavoring to grasp a desirable result in its completed form, without having worked to bring about the result and even without having given any particular intelligent consideration to the method of producing the desired result.

In the early days of machinery the ultimate judgment was decided, not upon the basis of the beauty of the machine, the cost of installation or upon any other feature of the particular machine, but upon its ability to produce a result. The main question was "Will it work?" This should be the question asked in regard to contemplated activities which are supposed to be for the welfare of the people. There are too many individuals at the present time who are anxious to experiment on the whole nation without first having tried out their particular formulas upon a small scale. Their contention is that it is impossible to try out certain things within the individual states and therefore such experiments must necessarily be national in scope. Here particularly is an example of misjudging values.

There are economic values that pertain to individual states, but there are also political, social and racial values that are extremely different in many of the states. There are relative degrees of state pride and of independence. To contend, therefore, that it is easier to experiment upon an entire nation composed of such diversified elements, rather than upon two or three individual states, which are comparatively unified in themselves, is to condemn the whole general theory of experimentation. If the experimenters have nothing better to offer than to make the entire nation a laboratory then it would be far better to remain as we are until a sounder system is established for finding out what the consequences of certain activities will actually be.

In our judgment of values in regard to things material, this can only be made progressive and substantial by acquiring further knowledge, discrimination and common sense. Each individual has certain tastes and inclinations which make some things more, or less, valuable to himself than to the majority of other individuals. This is as it should be. It would be rather unfortunate if we all wanted just exactly the same particular things.

In general, however, it can be said that the average man, in fact every man living, desires certain things regardless of his social standing, his business status or his age.

These things are:

First, sufficient food, clothing and shelter to be comfortable.

Second, a sufficient income for the actual needs of himself and his family.

Third, the right to choose his occupation, his place of business and his residence.

Fourth, freedom from interference with his religion, his right of free speech and his ability to reach the ear of authority.

Fifth, political freedom to wage a fair and square political battle against his opponents, with neither party having special privileges.

Sixth, entire absence of interference with his freedom of movement, with his method of conducting business, or with any of his personal activities, except such as might be harmful to others.

All of these objectives are desirable but the methods by which they are to be obtained should also be desirable, otherwise results will never be beneficial.

It is very important to remember that if we do evil in order to bring about a good result that the result will also be evil in its effect upon us. There is no method in a country such as our own to bring about changes that are for the benefit of society merely through the making of laws by a few individuals who happen to be in power. Such benefits can only come when the nation, by a large majority, concurs in and favors not only the result to be obtained but the methods by which such attainment shall be made possible. This must not only be true, but it also is important and vital that the minority be not actively against the methods that are to be pursued.

It is unfortunate that the question of public welfare has attached itself to the two great political parties. Public welfare should be bettered by careful, painstaking and scientific research which would actually reveal the consequences of a certain course of action and which would prove whether the result to be obtained could be accomplished by the suggested action.

In conclusion there are many other values which should always be maintained. The values of ideals and principles must always come first, but we have also the values of our loved ones, our friends and associates, our business companions and our social acquaintances. If we would only learn to use our judgment of values based entirely upon the method to be used in securing a result, and the honor, stability of character and common sense of the method, rather than the result itself; and if we would also learn to judge the value of our friends and fellow citizens by the same standards of honor, character, common sense and their methods and manner, then we would not be at all disappointed in the result that we achieved from our activities, or the happiness that we receive from merely living in the world with the kind of friends and fellow citizens with which we have enriched our own lives; and incidentally made ourselves better and stronger individuals, and we would have brought something worth while into the lives of other individuals and into that of the nation.

July, 1936

FAIR PLAY

THE ability to play fair is not inherent in the character of individuals but must be cultivated and must grow just as any other process of education. It involves not only a sound sense of justice, but also a reasonable amount of good judgment and an ability to maintain self-control and to avoid personal prejudice for or against individuals. In other words fair play results from the right attitude of an individual fully as much as from his actions.

The Golden Rule requires that we should do unto others as we would have them do to us, but it can readily be understood that if we would like others to render us more than justice and to give us things that we have not earned, that we would then be very injudicious and unwise in trying to follow the example of the Golden Rule. The Golden Rule presumes an intelligent understanding of what we should expect from others and it is this application of the Golden Rule that is important.

If we could learn to think in terms of fair play, which means that you expect nothing less than justice and fairness from your friends, and nothing more than the same things from your enemies, as well as from other individuals who are not included in either classification.

Much has been said of fair play as it involves other individuals, but little consideration has been given to the necessity of an individual playing fair with himself. For instance, the average boy and man start out with fair intentions and it could almost be taken for granted that practically all individuals would prefer to play fair. In certain circumstances, however, the problem of financial gain, of business advancement, or the attainment of some personally important objective induces individuals to take unfair advantage of other individuals along certain lines. In doing this they are being false to their own true character and their code of ethics, and a continuation along these lines would ultimately result in an absolute change of character and a complete abandonment of their code of ethics.

In this connection it should be remembered that a code of ethics is not an individual possession, that there is not one code of ethics for one individual and another code of ethics for another individual. It is not possible for an individual to choose certain principles to follow and call it a code of ethics unless these principles embrace all of the traits of character and codes of conduct that are necessary to make him dependable and reliable.

A man cannot say that he will avoid murder, burglary, robbery, and many other of the gravest crimes, but reserve the right to deceive people in certain ways that will bring him profits or benefits.

Every man is bound to make mistakes as to questions of judgment and justice in the course of his life. All of us will commit acts that are wrong or unwise, sometimes intentionally and other times without recognizing our shortcomings. But the important element to consider has to do with the intention of the man, the method and manner of his act, and the desire afterwards to correct his mistakes or to atone for any damage inflicted upon others.

We are not all gifted with the ability to judge quickly and clearly, especially in times of emotional crises, but our real intentions can always be measured by the efforts that we make to remedy our mistakes and to make up for our shortcomings and our departure from our code of ethics. However, most of our speech and actions are reasonably calculated and thought out beforehand and it can safely be said that under normal conditions the average man who has the sincere intent to play fair can find both the good judgment and sense of justice that will enable him to do so.

The greatest obstacle in the path of the average man arises from a distorted personal viewpoint due to love, affection, friendship and personal liking for certain individuals, as well as to suspicion, contempt, aversion, dislike, and sometimes even hatred in his attitude toward other individuals. It is hard to be just and fair as between a person that we love and another individual that we dislike, and yet it is possible for the average man to be fair under such conditions by removing from his mind the personality of the individuals affected.

If he would merely take the circumstances themselves, the speech and action to be considered and substitute in his mind two other individuals in whom he is not interested he would then be able to be fair in his judgment of the situation. The real obstacle does not lie in the inability of a man to be fair under such conditions but in the lack of desire on his part for fair play. He wants to believe that the person he loves is in the right and that the person that he dislikes is in the wrong and, this desire being in his heart, it is comparatively easy for him to be unfair from the standpoint of justice as well as good judgment.

If we could only realize that we take our friends and our loved ones as they are, with their faults as well as their virtues, and that we do not have to pretend to ourselves that their mistakes and wrongful actions should be condoned in order to preserve the friendship. In other words we do not have to believe that everything that our friends do is right. They can still be excellent friends and still do many things that are wrong, just as we ourselves may do.

On the other hand, because we recognize wrongful 'acts and condemn the act does not mean that we condemn our friends also. We should never acknowledge that a wrong is right because it is committed by someone we love, but we should also never condemn someone we love because of minor faults and shortcomings. If we really and truly love someone or have a deep friendship for someone, we actually harm them by exhibiting favoritism and trying to benefit them at the expense of others.

We have a perfect right to give freely to those we love, but not in such a manner or in a way that will render them weak, inefficient, dependent or irresponsible. When we do such things we are not playing fair with our friends and loved ones. We are teaching them to be weak instead of strong, whereas we should impart whatever strength of character we are able to transmit to those we love, so that they may become as strong and as self-reliant as ourselves, if not more so. Especially is this true with those individuals who seem to be most helpless, our children.

Almost from babyhood a child should be taught to be as self-reliant as its capabilities will permit. A child's character should be strengthened by every possible reasonable method that parents can think of. Children should be taught from an early age to play fair and to be able to enjoy games and sports if they lose, practically as much as if they win.

It is comparatively easy to teach children these things as they are very adaptive and almost super-intelligent in detecting sincerity and soundness of judgment in the advice that is given them. It might be said that the only thing necessary is for the parents to have the proper viewpoint themselves and the sincere desire to make their children strong and self-reliant.

Many parents actually help to keep their children dependent on the parents; they try to fight the children's battles for them instead of teaching them the proper thing to do under certain conditions that arise. They want to take the part of their own children as against other children and it is often true that this very attitude of the parents would indicate that their own children were in the wrong instead of their playmates about whom they complain.

Children must be taught that at certain times and under certain conditions they will meet with injustice and oppression from other individuals who are stronger, more powerful, more dominating or more fortunately situated than themselves, and that their problem is not to bring these other individuals down to their own level, from the standpoint of force or strength, but to be able to rise above such individuals and to either hold their own with them or to intelligently avoid further association.

In thinking about children's problems in this respect it must always be remembered that some of the so-called nicest children turn out to be terrible "flops" as adult men and women, while on the other hand, a certain boy who might have acquired the reputation of being the most annoying boy in the neighborhood might turn out to be one of the finest young men in the community. Final judgment therefore should not be rendered against children because of unfortunate conditions that may cause them to be mischievous and troublesome. At the same time care should be taken to see that our own children do not acquire the habits and the attitude of such other children while they are in such transition periods.

American citizens are fortunate in having an inheritance of good sports and games of skill, and it therefore should not require anything more than careful attention to carry these same principles and ethics into our other relations with people in our other activities. In teaching our children to be strong and self-reliant one of our greatest helps will be to teach them to think of other activities in life in the same way as they do their sports and games.

Practically nothing else is really required to induce the average child to play fair and they can probably understand what fair play means to a far greater extent than their parents would believe possible.

However, it must never be forgotten that the parents must themselves set an example of fair play for their children to follow, for children are far more likely to emulate their parents' example than they are to follow their advice, especially when the advice and the example fail to coincide. Fair play in the game of life necessitates a code of ethics translated into rules and regulations that are readily understandable. In a future message these rules and regulations will be expounded under a code of fair play for the education and the understanding of each of us as individuals.

The ability to play fair is a cardinal virtue. Without it, a man cannot hope for real success or happiness. With it, he can not only count on success and happiness, but he can also count on the respect and friendship of his fellow men and the satisfaction and pride that comes to every man who knows he has helped many and harmed no one, and has brought happiness and pleasure to his loved ones.

August, 1936

"Walter Grass Jr."